THE VERY LARGE CHURCH

Lyle E. Schaller

The Very Large Church

Abingdon Press
Nashville

THE VERY LARGE CHURCH

This book is printed on recycled, acid-free, elemental-chlorine free paper.

Library of Congress Cataloging-in-Publication Data

Schaller, Lyle E.
  The very large church: is it in your future / Lyle E. Schaller.
     p. cm.
  Includes bibliographical references.
  ISBN 0-687-09045-8 (alk. paper)
  1. Big churches.   I. Title.

BV637.9 .S34 2000
254—dc21   99-044994

To

Mary and Ezra Earl Jones

02 03 04 05 06 07 08 09—10 9 8 7 6

MANUFACTURED IN THE UNITED STATES OF AMERICA

Contents

Introduction

In May 1937 I graduated from the Hickory Park Elementary School, a tax-supported public school located on a one-acre campus three miles south of Lime Ridge, Wisconsin. The campus included four white wood buildings. The largest was a one-room (two, if you count the entry area, which also served as the cloakroom) building that contained 32 desks for students, plus the large teacher's desk and a bookcase that contained the 200-volume school library.

The second largest building was a woodshed that contained the supply of hardwood used to fire the furnace in the school basement. After playing in the wet snow, standing over that hot air register in the middle of the room was a memorable way to dry off and warm up. The other two structures were small privies; the one south of the woodshed was for girls and the one to the north for boys. The campus also included two steel swings, a softball diamond, a well with a hand-operated pump, and a dozen trees.

By definition, the teacher's role was as a generalist who taught all subjects from art to history to music and spelling, but who also served as the chief administrator, disciplinarian, coach, custodian, surrogate parent, arbitrator of disputes, school nurse, playground supervisor, director of the annual Christmas pageant, and counselor.

For eight years it was, next to the family, the center of life for the 28 to 32 children enrolled in one of the eight grades. That school district, which was an independent unit of local government, covered an area approximately two miles by three miles in size that included three dozen farms.

The graduating class of 1934 was taught by the nineteen-year-old son of one of those families. He had graduated with the eighth graders of 1928 and, therefore, had been an older schoolmate of some of the class of 1934. After four years in a nearby high school and a year at the county normal (teacher training) school, located fifteen miles from his home (but far beyond commuting distance), he returned to teach for three years at his alma mater. Several years later he earned his doctorate and became a university professor.

The one-room country school was a wonderful invention! It facilitated peer learning, encouraged egalitarianism, rewarded merit, modeled respect for legitimate authority, emphasized the three R's, and reinforced the need to master skills in interpersonal relationships. With a typical enrollment between 15 and 32, it encouraged one-to-one relationships between teacher and learner. It was as large as a social network can be and still retain the luxuries of intimacy and simplicity. It also was the ideal institution for socializing the children and grandchildren of the immigrants from Western Europe into the culture, political system, economy, language, and labor force of the United States.

It was small enough, in terms of the number of students, for an easy transition from the family nest into a larger social setting. The typical first grader already knew a majority of the student body before that scary first day of school.

In 1935, incidentally, the total dollar cost of operating the Hickory Park School averaged out to approximately $30 per pupil for the year. (That would be the equivalent of approximately $500 in 2000 terms after allowing for inflation. In 1935, $30 was two weeks' salary for an experienced elementary school teacher. In 2000, $500 was two days' salary for an experienced elementary school teacher.)

After eight years in that small friendly, supportive, intimate, relatively simple, easy-to-comprehend, and substantially homogeneous social setting, most of us entered into a more intimidating, far more complex, less user friendly, more competitive, and heterogeneous environment called high school.

These institutions typically employed three to ten full-time adults, most of them specialists who were comfortable explaining what did not fit into their job description. A few accepted the role of surrogate parent, friend, or counselor, but usually with only a tiny number of students. English teacher, coach, principal, bus driver, custodian, and science teacher communicated that they were specialists, not generalists. Likewise, the grade a pupil was in further fragmented the student body. In the one-room country school, the fifth and sixth graders frequently functioned as one class, but in high school, many of the seniors never bothered to learn to identify all the freshmen and sophomores correctly by name.

The village high school of 1940 operated with a radically different rule book from the one that was used in the one-room rural school of that day.

That design of the public school system in rural and small-town America was mirrored by much of American Protestantism. The countryside was covered with the buildings housing small congregations that averaged 7 to 40 at worship. Many were able to provide an even more supportive and reassuring social setting than were those one-room schools. They perpetuated their Western European heritage by sharpening the distinctive identity with both a denominational and a nationality image. That is a Norwegian Lutheran parish. That is a German Evangelical church. That is a Dutch Reformed congregation. That is a Swedish Methodist church. That is a Welsh Presbyterian church.

The rural and small-town social systems were designed to allow children to move out of the close intimacy of the family setting into a relatively simple and easy-to-comprehend elementary school before being challenged to master the skills required to function effectively in large groups that included more than forty people.[1] It was not until after one's seventeeth or eighteenth birthday that a young person was expected to be comfortable in a social setting that included several hundred to a few thousand people.

Six decades after four of us eighth graders graduated from

11

Hickory Park School, the public school district west of where we now live constructed a new building. It is designed to accommodate 800 four-year-old children in the prekindergarten program offered by that district.

From the Civil War through the Great Depression, American society prepared children to learn how to live in a world of small institutions that placed a high value on intimacy, simplicity, small numbers, and mutual support. It was not until becoming a teenager that one was forced to master the skills required for life in a more anonymous, complex, and hostile social environment.

Imagine the experience of a six-year-old starting first grade in a building with 20 to 30 other children, one or two of whom may be siblings, three or four relatives, and several friends or acquaintances. Compare that with the experience of the four-year-old entering for the first time into a school building filled with 799 other four-year-olds plus the scores of adult strangers required to staff that enterprise!

From the Civil War through the Great Depression, American society prepared children to learn how to live in a world of small institutions that placed a high value on intimacy, simplicity, small numbers, and mutual support. It was not until becoming a teenager that one was forced to master the skills required for life in a more anonymous, complex, and hostile social environment. (That generalization applied not only to the rural United States in the first half of the twentieth century, but also to many central city neighborhoods, especially those with a high level of ethnic homogeneity, that also were organized around intimacy, spontaneity, simplicity, and small private institutions [retail stores, clubs, lodges, service providers, etc.].)

That culture was comfortable with the small to middle-sized Protestant congregation averaging fewer than 135 at worship. At this point, it may be worth noting that in 1929–30, when I was a first grader, there were 150,000 one-teacher public elementary schools in the United States, down from slightly over 200,000 in 1916. By the time I graduated in 1937, that number had dropped to 125,000, and it plunged to 35,000 in 1956. Today there are fewer than 100 one-teacher public schools.

In 1930 the 262,000 public schools in the United States enrolled 26 million pupils in twelve grades, an average of 100 students per school. Seventy years later, the 80,000 public elementary and high schools in America enrolled 48 million students in grades K–12, an average of 600 per school.

Concurrently, the average (mean) size of a Protestant congregation in the United States tripled between 1906 and 1996.

As late as the 1950s and 1960s, many denominational ministerial placement systems operated on the same basic assumption. Regardless of one's age or personal history, the best entry point into the pastoral ministry was first to serve a small single-cell congregation organized around a network of one-to-one relationships, kinfolk ties, intimacy, simplicity, local traditions, a denominational identity, and the maintenance of a meeting place. That was widely perceived as a useful prerequisite to prepare a minister to move on to a large multicell congregation filled with complexity,

This new culture organized around big institutions is governed by a different rule book from that which was used in the old culture composed largely of small institutions.

anonymity, and a more highly structured organizational system.

Why write a book on the role and future of the large church? One reason is that the culture has been transformed. Instead of preparing children for life in a world of small institutions, for the past half century the American culture has been equipping people to live in a world of big institutions. This new culture organized around big institutions is governed by a different rule book from that which was used in the old culture composed largely of small institutions.

This autobiographical account illustrates the changing context for ministry as well as for public education. The educational requirements to be a public school teacher or a parish pastor are far greater today than they were in the 1930s. The support system for public schools or for the parish ministry is weaker than it once was. The era of small institutions has been replaced by a day when most of the participants are found in the big institutions. The day of the generalist has been replaced by the demand for specialists. The expectations people project on the church or the public school are far greater today than formerly. The total annual compensation for both the parish pastor and the public school teacher has increased at a faster rate than the increase in per capita income. The public schools and the parish church are faced with more competition for the loyalty of their constituents than ever before. The public schools and the churches were widely viewed as allies and potential partners in the first half of the twentieth century. By the end of the century, they often were viewed as adversaries. Both the neighborhood school and the neighborhood church have been placed on the endangered species list. In recent years, hundreds of books have been published that are highly critical of contemporary public education or of the contemporary parish ministry. The schools that train future public school teachers or future parish pastors often are the subject of condescending comments and ridicule by many professors in the elite research universities. Newspaper stories about the public schools or the Christian churches in the large central cities often make repeated use of the words *failure* and *renewal.* Service as a public school teacher or as a parish pastor, once widely perceived to be a lifelong career, often is an interlude today between graduation from a professional school and entrance into the secular labor force. The leaders in public schools and in many of the denominationally affiliated congregations feel that their work is increasingly regulated by distant bureaucrats who "do not understand what life is like here in the trenches." Both public school systems and ecclesiastical organizations offer a more attractive reward for administrators than for those who are involved firsthand in serving the constituency the organization originally was created to serve. In both vocations a common contemporary comment is, "We are no longer able to attract the high-quality candidates for our vocation that we once did." In both the public schools and the parish churches, the generations born after 1945 want a broader range of choices, and this gives an unprecedented advantage to the large institutions. In the typical community, the role of public school teacher or parish pastor does not bring with it the automatic respect and deference it once carried. Much of what volunteers did in earlier decades is now being done by paid staff.

The reader can add another dozen examples of how the societal context has changed for both the public schools and the parish ministry. In both areas of life, however, the basic point is the same. The past several decades have been marked by an unprecedented degree of discontinuity with the past. Part of that discontinuity is reflected in the new rule book on how to do church in the new millennium.

This autobiographical account also is offered to illustrate two other points. The first is the ambivalence felt by many of us who grew up in a culture dominated by small social insti-

15

tutions. Our hearts are with the small school, the small church, the "Mom and Pop" grocery store, the one-screen motion picture theater, the physician in solo practice working out of his house, the corner druggist, and the family farm. Our heads, however, tell us that the future is with the large complex and anonymous institutions, such as the thirty-screen motion picture theater, the medical clinic with a staff of forty or more physicians, the three-acre building housing that new home supply and hardware store, the 100,000-square-foot supermarket, and the megachurch averaging over a thousand in worship every week. We are torn between what we like and what meets our needs. Earlier in life we learned how to be comfortable with the old rule book. Now we are being told we must follow a new set of rules.

Second, while the future is filled with uncertainty, most of the contemporary evidence suggests that the people born after 1965, who were socialized into adulthood in a culture dominated by big institutions, will outlive those born before 1945 who carry happy firsthand memories of a culture dominated by small institutions. In planning for the future of your congregation, do you expect most of your new members in the 2000–2020 era will be people born before 1945 or after 1965?

For those who want to be advised of the central thesis of a book before deciding whether to read it, this volume has three. *One is the need for more very large congregations if the goal is to confront the generations born after 1965 with the truth and relevance of the Christian gospel.* The second is that it requires an affirmation of the fact that the megachurch is not simply an overgrown version of a big congregation averaging 450 to 700 at worship—it is a sharply different order of God's creation! That is why a new rule book is needed.

Third, while the first half of the twentieth century was supportive of small institutions, the early years of the third millennium provide a context that is supportive of big institutions. The most important single component of this new context often is described as consumerism. Consumerism has changed the rules of the game!

A simple way to describe this is that the small churches, those averaging fewer than a hundred at worship, play by their own rules on their distinctive playing field. Another 40-plus percent, those averaging 100 to 700 at worship, use a different rule book that is appropriate for their playing field. The 3 to 5 percent that either average 800 or more at worship or have the potential to be in that size bracket use the most recent edition of a different rule book and play on a much larger field that is not restricted by geographical boundaries.

This book was written for those congregational leaders, both volunteer and paid staff, who recognize that their old rule book is obsolete and who are eager to learn how to participate effectively in the very large church game on a playing field that is defined by the culture, the societal context, clearly defined expectations, a theological belief system, a passion for evangelism, a high level of competence, creativity, innovation, and a new and different set of rules, rather than by local traditions or geographical boundaries or yesterday's stereotypes.

The new millennium has brought a new game to town that requires the players to master a new rule book.

CHAPTER ONE

Culture, Size, and Certainty

W hat is the crucial difference between, on the one
hand, the United States Army, the United States
Air Force, and the United States Navy, and, on
the other hand, the United States Marine Corps? According
to military journalist Thomas E. Ricks, the answer is in the
cultures.[1] To a substantial degree, the Army, the Air Force,
and the Navy are organized around their "toys" and the training of people to use these toys. These include battleships,
tanks, air-to-ground missiles, fighter planes, submarines, hel-
icopters, strategies for fighting two wars concurrently,
bombers, weapons carriers, doctrines, and rules.

By contrast, the Marine Corps is organized around a deep
and rich culture that has "a deep anchor in [its] own history
and mythology." Ricks adds that "the Marines stand out as a
successful and healthy institution that unabashedly teaches
values . . . to the bottom half of American society."[2] The rule
book used by the Marine Corps is consistent with the culture.

After hitting the bottom in the 1970s in terms of morale,
quality of recruits, and race relations, Ricks contends, the
Marines have rebounded and now stand out as the best of the
four branches of the American military services. That
rebound is due in large measure to a renewed emphasis on
doing what they do best. Instead of begging for more money
to buy new toys, the Marines have exploited their culture—
values, assumptions, and traditions—to transform recruits
into Marines and individuals into cohesive and effective fighting units. This emphasis on culture and values is reflected in
the themes emphasized by the Marine Corps in recruiting
volunteers. The other three branches of the military services

focus on consumerism—What's in it for me if I enlist? Technical training? Educational benefits? Early retirement? An excellent pension system? Travel? By contrast, the Marines focus on challenging recruits to fulfill their potential.

The culture of the Marine Corps includes projecting high expectations on both recruits and units, the transmission of values (honor, courage, faithfulness, commitment, fidelity, and integrity), minimizing racial and social class differences, the integration of those values into a way of life, and an acceptance of the fact that some will drop out, but that does not justify lowering the standards.

THE HIGH-EXPECTATION CULTURE

What are the basic differences between the typical American Protestant congregation of today and those churches that project high expectations of anyone who wants to become a full member? One answer is in the cultures.

As the decades roll by, the culture of the typical congregation increasingly reflects local traditions, the values, priorities in ministry, the expectations of what the future will bring shared by the committee members (who may have died seventy years ago) responsible for the design of the meeting place, the theological stance, and priorities of one or two long-tenured pastors, the expectations brought by the most influential contemporary volunteer leaders, and the doctrine and polity of that religious tradition. Taking good care of today's members, transmitting the faith to the next generation, balancing expenditures with income, maintaining the real estate, perpetuating local customs, and seeking replacements for the members who leave become high priorities. Among the other goals are enlisting volunteers, encouraging members to be better stewards of both time and money, and persuading people to attend special events and to contribute money for missions.

The natural, normal, and predictable institutional tendency is to create a new worshiping community to proclaim the gospel to the unchurched. But gradually the emphasis shifts to a focus on how to persuade people to be more supportive of that congregation.

The culture of the high-expectation churches tends to resemble that of the Marine Corps. The initial focus is on persuading the nonbeliever of the relevance and truth of the Christian faith. The culture of the Marines includes the basic assumption that "every recruit . . . has the ability to become a United States Marine." The culture of the high-expectation church includes the basic assumption that every human being can and should become a fully devoted follower of Jesus Christ.

The culture of the high-expectation churches tends to resemble that of the Marine Corps. The initial focus is on persuading the nonbeliever of the relevance and truth of the Christian faith. The culture of the Marines Includes the basic assumption that "every recruit . . . has the ability to become a United States Marine." The culture of the high-expectation church includes the basic assumption that every human being can and should become a fully devoted follower of Jesus Christ.

The training program for prospective Marines includes the assumption that recruits must be transformed from isolated, consumer-driven, and self-centered individuals into warriors as the first step in the sequence. Next they must learn to identify with a unit and automatically act in the best interests of that unit, rather than in their own self-interest. That transformation requires time; the following of a tested discipline;

emphasis on the challenge of meeting high expectations and doing what they know is beyond their capabilities; participation in a mutual support system; integration into the assumptions, beliefs, and values of the Marine culture; and leads eventually to acceptance as a full member of that special set-apart group.

The Marine Corps has been especially successful with recruits who come from the lower socio-educational-economic half of the young adult population.

Today's high-expectation churches act on a parallel set of assumptions. Instead of emphasizing a member's obligation to support that congregation, these worshiping communities concentrate on helping individuals progress from skeptic or seeker to believer to learner to disciple to apostle. They challenge every pilgrim to fulfill the disciplines of a group designed to transform believers into disciples. These high-expectation churches challenge nonbelievers, skeptics, pilgrims, and new believers to become what they knew was impossible for them. The high-expectation churches follow a different rule book from that used in low-expectation congregations.

WHAT'S THE POINT?

The differences in the institutional culture are the key to understanding why at the end of the twentieth century the Marine Corps differed so greatly from the other three branches of the United States military system.

Likewise, the differences in the religious culture are the most significant line of demarcation that separates one group of Protestant congregations from another larger group of churches. One consequence of those differences in congregational cultures is the recent increase in the number of very large Protestant congregations in the United States. This can be illustrated by seven questions.

1. Why have so many congregations plateaued in size

with an average worship attendance in the 500 to 700 range rather than continuing to grow?

One part of the explanation is that the leaders were content to attempt to perpetuate the congregational culture that is appropriate for a large church rather than revise it to a set of assumptions, values, and expectations appropriate for a megachurch.

2. Why have so many congregations that once averaged 800 to 3,000 at worship shrunk to a much smaller size?

Instead of "acting their size," they decided to act like a middle-sized or large congregation and created a self-fulfilling prophecy. Frequently this coincided with the arrival of a new senior pastor who brought a congregational culture appropriate for a smaller church.

3. A disproportionately large number of contemporary megachurches were either (a) founded after 1970 or (b) relocated their meeting place after 1970. Why is that the pattern?

Most, but not all, relocations are motivated by a desire to reach a new constituency. Most, but not all, new missions were and are founded to reach unchurched people. In both cases this means creating a congregational culture—values, assumptions, and priorities—that is focused on helping the individual on a self-identified personal and spiritual pilgrimage move in the direction of becoming a fully devoted follower of Jesus Christ. The institutional needs of that congregation become a relatively low priority.

Many of the megachurches of the 1950s and 1960s drifted away from that earlier emphasis on responding to the religious needs of the people and moved institutional goals to the top of the list of priorities. That was followed eventually by a decline in the size of the constituency.

One common consequence was that the average worship attendance gradually became a smaller and smaller fraction of the reported membership.

In the relatively new high-commitment congregation, the reported membership may be only one-third or one-fourth of the average weekly worship attendance. "Everyone is welcome to worship with us and to participate in the learning opportunities we offer, but the threshold for becoming a member is very high."

A parallel characteristic is that the number-one criterion for enlisting volunteers is, "Will this help that person progress to the next stage of his or her personal and spiritual pilgrimage?" It is not, "Who will fill that empty slot in our table of organization?"

4. Which of the 300,000-plus Protestant congregations in the United States are most attractive to people seeking a new church home?

Those that project high expectations of people on a self-identified religious pilgrimage tend to be more attractive, especially to the generations born after World War II, than those that project low expectations.

5. Which are the least attractive?

The least attractive are those that seek new members primarily because of the pressures of institutional survival and/or to enlist people to help fulfill congregational or denominational goals.

6. What is one of the most difficult assignments challenging a pastor today?

High on that list is the challenge to lead in the merger of two long-established small congregations, each with its own distinctive culture and each with a recent history of the members' growing older in age and fewer in numbers. The motivation for the merger is to combine the assets of the two congregations in order to attract younger generations of members and/or to become a large regional church, but frequently little attention is devoted to the cultural conflicts that usually undermine that strategy.

7. What does all of this have to do with the increase in

the number of megachurches and the need for more very large congregations?

While size is the most highly visible characteristic of the very large congregation, size is really (a) a product of the culture of that congregation, not an end in itself, and (b) is of secondary importance when compared to the congregational culture.

One simplification of this point is that the leaders in the congregation averaging 500 to 700 in weekly worship, and that is located in an environment that would be compatible with doubling or tripling in size, probably will have to make substantial changes in the culture to translate that opportunity into reality.

A second is those who go to spend two or three or four days studying a megachurch in order to learn how to "do church better back home" would be well advised to seek to understand the unique culture of that teaching church, rather than simply to focus on methods and techniques.

A third implication is that the minister or lay program staff member moving from a large church to one averaging a thousand or more at worship should recognize that the change in cultures may be greater than if one moved from a large church in one denomination to a large church in a different religious tradition.

Perhaps the most important implication can be summarized in the word *intentionality.* In the ideal world, the culture of a particular congregation is appropriate for (a) the size of that congregation, (b) the current environment in which that congregation finds itself, and (c) what the leaders are convinced the Lord is calling that worshiping community to be and to be doing in the next three to seven years.

One highly visible negative example is the open country church in rural America founded in 1890 that averaged 30 to 45 at worship for several decades. In the 1970s, residential subdivisions and commercial developments began to replace the farms. The number of people living within two or three miles of the meeting place increased from 100 to several thousand. A new mission meeting in a building a half mile away averages 600 at worship, but that small, rural, culture-bound church now averages only 25 at worship.

A second example is the neighborhood church founded by an Anglo denomination in 1925 to serve newcomers to a new residential subdivision. It peaked in size in 1955. Recent immigrants to the United States moved into that neighborhood in large numbers in the 1970s and 1980s, and that congregation celebrated its sixtieth birthday by dissolving and selling the real estate to an immigrant group.

Culture, size, and change are three of the themes that run through this book and that deserve the attention of the leaders in very large churches.

THE NEW ENEMY?

For well over a century the leaders in small Protestant congregations have had to defend their continued existence. Back in the 1880s, Washington Gladden was one of the most outspoken critics of the excessive number of small Protestant worshiping communities. The reformers who led this attack on the small church—and the primary focal point was on small rural congregations—peaked in influence in the 1920–60 era.[3]

In recent years, the pendulum has swung back, and today it is the megachurch that is the focal point of the ecclesiastical critics. These critics include municipal officials who object to taking a sixty-acre parcel of land off the tax roll to house a congregation averaging 4,500 at worship—but do not object to a congregation averaging 300 at worship purchasing a five-acre church site. These critics include pastors and volunteer leaders from small and middle-sized congregations who are convinced that there is a finite number of churchgoers out there and that the megachurch is attracting an unfair share of that market. These critics include residents living nearby who object to the construction of a physical facility that may bring a couple of thousand strangers into their sparsely populated residential neighborhood two or three times every week. They also object to the increase in the volume of traffic on nearby streets or that new construction may require cutting down seventy-year-old trees or paving over what is now green grass or that will change the view from the picture window in their living room. Many of the founding pastors of today's megachurches are not graduates of accredited theological schools. Their critics include scholars who perceive the emergence of the American megachurch as a deplorable break with Western European religious practices. Many of these critics also object to a rule book that governs the policy decisions of the very large churches.

In the face of these and other criticisms, why would anyone suggest a need for more very large congregations? Why should congregations now averaging 350 to 700 at worship be encouraged to double or triple or quadruple in size? Why switch from the old model in planting new missions by gathering 25 to 75 adults as the nucleus to a large church model that is designed to produce a congregation averaging at least 700 at worship by the end of year seven?

SEVEN ASSUMPTIONS

Before moving into a discussion of why there is a need for more very large congregations, it may help to identify seven basic assumptions on which this book is based.

First, it is assumed that next to the congregational culture, size is the most revealing and useful frame of reference for examining the differences among congregations in American Protestantism.[4]

Second, the average weekly attendance in worship is the

most reliable yardstick to use in measuring size. For this discussion, a simple five-category classification system is used.

FIVE TYPES OF CHURCHES

Size	Average Worship Attendance
Small	up to 100
Midsize	101 to 350
Large	351 to 750
Very Large	751 to 1,800
Megachurch	1,801 plus

The number-one deficiency in this system is placing the congregation averaging 115 at worship in the same category with one averaging 335, but that group is not the focus of this book.[5] The two arguments for collapsing what really are at least nine categories into five are that (a) most of us normal people have difficulty keeping track of nine categories in our head and (b) the second most crucial line of demarcation in defining patterns of institutional behavior is between churches averaging under 700 to 750 at worship and those averaging 800 or more. (The most critical line of demarcation is between small congregations with a full-time resident pastor and small churches served by a part-time minister.)

A third assumption is that the normative size for a worshiping community in American Protestantism is approximately 35 to 40 at worship. When a congregation exceeds that number, the natural, normal, and predictable institutional pressures begin to work in the direction of reducing that number. Thus the larger the size of the congregation, the more fragile it is in institutional terms.[6]

Fourth, the longer a congregation has been meeting in the same building at the same location, the more powerful are the traditions, values, and habits that are rooted in the past. This

28

helps to explain why such a large proportion of contemporary megachurches either were founded after 1970 or relocated to a new meeting place since 1970. New institutions are more likely to be open to innovation than are old institutions. Congregations that have voted once for radical change (relocation of the meeting place) are more likely to be open to innovation than are congregations that have never embarked on the road to radical change.

The fifth basic assumption is a projection from the twentieth century into the third millennium. Churches are larger than they used to be, and that trend will continue. In 1906 a census of churches conducted by the United States Bureau of the Census revealed the average (mean) size of a Roman Catholic parish was 969 baptized souls—a remarkable increase from the 1890 average of 610. In 1996 the (mean) average size of a Roman Catholic parish in the United States was 2,692 baptized members, more than quadruple the 1890 average.

In 1906 the 12,703 Lutheran congregations in the United States reported an average of 166 baptized members per parish, up from 143 in 1890. In 1996 the 17,800 Lutheran congregations reported an average of 445 baptized members, nearly triple the average of ninety years earlier.

For various Presbyterian denominations, the (mean) average size rose from 95 members in 1890 to 118 in 1906 to 295 for the 15,000 Presbyterian congregations of 1996—triple the 1890 average.

In 1906 the six predecessor denominations of The United Methodist Church reported a combined total of 5.3 million members scattered among 57,084 congregations, for an average of 93 members per church. In 1965, the two predecessor denominations reported a combined total of 43,032 congregations with 11,081,000 members, or an average of 257 members per church. By 1996 that had dropped to an average of 234 members in 36,300 congregations.

Like grocery stores, medical clinics, universities, airlines, farms, discount stores, financial institutions, and elementary schools, churches are larger than they used to be.

A sixth and central assumption is that the differences among Protestant congregations today are greater and more significant than they were as recently as the 1950s. These differences include staffing, ideology, governance, self-image, finances, priorities in ministry, theological stance, and goals. They are discussed in more detail in subsequent chapters.

Finally, and this runs completely counter to the assumptions of many ecclesiastical leaders, it is assumed that ideologically liberal institutions naturally generate more resistance to proposed change in practices than is the pattern of ideologically conservative institutions. For example, an ideologically conservative president, Richard M. Nixon, was able to advocate the formal recognition of Red China.

Most of us need a point of dependable stability and continuity in our lives. The ideologically conservative finds that point of stability and predictability in ideology and thus is free to advocate change in practices and institutional life. The ideological liberal is more open to new ideas and innovation in ideology and thus looks for continuity, predictability, and stability in practices and institutional life.

One contemporary example is that most university faculty

members are ideologically liberal, but oppose the innovation described as distance learning. A second is that changes in worship usually gain widespread approval sooner in theologically conservative congregations than in theologically liberal churches. A third is in the creation of a multicultural congregation. That usually is easiest in the theologically very conservative charismatic fellowships and far more difficult in the theologically liberal church that is committed to a Western European approach to worship and to a high degree of diversity in theology.

When this last assumption is combined with the fact that most new missions founded since 1970 were launched by evangelicals, that helps to explain why such a large proportion of today's very large churches are on the conservative side of the theological spectrum.

WHY MORE VERY LARGE CHURCHES?

These assumptions will help the reader to understand the context for urging an increase in the number of very large churches. In simple pragmatic terms, the answer to that "Why?" question begins with distinguishing between the gospel of Jesus Christ and the vessel in which it is transmitted from one generation to the next. If the goal is to reach, attract, welcome, serve, include, assimilate, and challenge the generations born after 1965, then that often means a congregation has to (1) excel in presenting the gospel in what is perceived as relevant terms (and that often includes growing weekday ministries); (2) be able to earn a reputation for high quality in worship, teaching, training, and other aspects of congregational life; and (3) provide people with a broad range of attractive choices in worship, learning, involvement in doing ministry, facilitating their individual personal spiritual pilgrimage, helping them rear their children, and finding a sense of community.

That threefold emphasis on relevance, quality, and choices requires a large base of resources. A generous estimate is that only one out of five of today's Protestant congregations can mobilize the resources required to meet all three of those expectations.

From an ideological perspective of those who are convinced of the desirability of more intergenerational and intercultural churches, the very large congregation is a central component of a larger strategy. This can be seen most clearly in worship where one service is designed for an older, English-speaking generation, another for a Spanish language constituency, a third for the American-born adult children of immigrant parents, a fourth for those who prefer a multimedia worship experience with contemporary Christian music, a fifth centered on the Eucharist and classical Christian music, and a sixth for those in intercultural marriages. That schedule is possible in the mega-church, but not in the small or midsize congregation.

> ✝
>
> If the goal is to reach, attract, welcome, serve, include, assimilate, and challenge the generations born after 1965, then that often means a congregation has to (1) excel in presenting the gospel in what is perceived as relevant terms (and that often includes growing weekday ministries); (2) be able to earn a reputation for high quality in worship, teaching, training, and other aspects of congregational life; and (3) provide people with a broad range of attractive choices in worship, learning, involvement in doing ministry, facilitating their individual personal spiritual pilgrimage, helping them rear their children, and finding a sense of community.

Those with a strong future orientation who also are open to change in religious practices point to a third contribution of the very large churches. Many of these congregations have emerged as the new research and development centers for American Christianity. Back in the 1950s the "new ways of doing church" were being invented by denominational agencies, theological schools, and a few parachurch organizations. Today most of that pioneering is being done by the very large teaching churches, a growing variety of parachurch organizations, and scores of entrepreneurial individuals.

A parallel defense of the need for more very large congregations can be introduced by a simple question: Who is best equipped to plant new missions? In the middle third of the twentieth century, it was widely assumed the answer was denominational agencies. The only serious difference of opinion was whether that should be the regional judicatories or the national denominational staff. One consequence was literally thousands of new missions that either closed before their tenth birthday or plateaued in size with an average worship attendance under 100.

Today there is a growing recognition that a crucial ingredient in planting new missions is an understanding of the differences between functioning as a large church that can attract and welcome newcomers and acting like a small congregation that concentrates on serving its present constituency.

Today there is a growing recognition that a crucial ingredient in planting new missions is an understanding of the differences between functioning as a large church that can attract and welcome newcomers and acting like a small congregation that concentrates on serving its present constituency. The best place to look for leaders, both volunteers and paid staff, who understand that distinction, is in the very large and numerically growing congregation. One result is the increasing proportion of new missions being planted by very large churches.

Overlapping these distinctive contributions is a fifth reason to advocate an increase in the number of very large churches. This can be introduced by a highly simplistic typology. For this discussion, congregations in American Protestantism can be divided into three categories. The largest number place taking care of today's members and/or institutional survival at the top of the priority list in the allocation of scarce resources, such as time, energy, money, building space, the weekly schedule, and creativity. Perhaps one-third could be called "congregation-building" churches. They place a high priority on expanding their ministry to reach potential future members. Possibly as many as 2 percent can be classified as "kingdom-building" churches. These congregations place a high priority on mobilizing resources that will be used to build God's kingdom in other parts of the world. Some of these efforts, such as sending 300 people and $300,000 to plant a new mission in a community a few miles away, may be viewed as inconsistent with a congregation-building strategy.

Where are we most effective in reaching the unchurched, the generations born after World War II, the church shoppers, the American-born adult children of recent immigrants, and those on a self-identified religious quest? In at least a dozen denominations the answer is, "In our new missions and our very largest congregations."

The need is for more kingdom-building churches, but it is rare for any except the very large congregations to be able to provide the discretionary resources required to fill that role.

A sixth and highly pragmatic reason for advocating more very large congregations is the ecclesiastical marketplace. From a denominational perspective, this can be stated very simply: Where are we most effective in reaching the unchurched, the generations born after World War II, the church shoppers, the American-born adult children of recent immigrants, and those on a self-identified religious quest? In at least a dozen denominations the answer is, "In our new missions and our very largest congregations."

The critics dismiss that as one more concession to consumerism, but that is the subject of chapter 3. The policy makers in the numerically shrinking denominations are confronted with five basic choices as they design a strategy for a new millennium:

1. Do we make the top priority in the allocation of scarce resources keeping the dying churches alive for as long as possible?

2. Do we focus our resources on planting new missions?

3. Do we concentrate our limited resources on encouraging an increase in the number of very large congregations?

4. Do we make the first two our top priorities and divide most of our discretionary resources between the two?

5. Do we watch passively as our constituency grows older in age and fewer in numbers? As that trend continues, do we concentrate a large share of our discretionary resources on issue-centered ministries (racism, poverty, human sexuality, etc.), on conflict resolution in congregational life, on denominational goals, on financial support for institutions founded before 1960, and on taking better care of the clergy? While we do that, other denominations and the independent churches will respond to that market demand for more very large congregations.

A seventh reason may be the second most controversial of all. The 1990s brought a technological revolution equivalent to the invention of movable type and the printing press in the fifteenth century. How do we proclaim the gospel to younger generations? One rapidly growing part of the answer is a shift from the printed and spoken word to visual communication, including drama, music, visual images, motion, and humor.

One strategy for responding to the challenges and opportunities brought by the new technology is to replace the traditional low-energy and relatively passive presentation-type worship service with a nontraditional, high-energy, and multimedia participatory worship experience. That is change by subtraction and is almost always disruptive. An alternative is change by addition. This calls for continuing the traditional worship service, ideally in the same room at the same hour, and adding one or two or three nontraditional worship experiences to the weekly schedule. Far fewer than one-third of all Protestant congregations can mobilize the resources required for that change-by-addition strategy.

Who will create the new models of nontraditional worship that others can study and perhaps adapt? Most will be either new missions or very large self-identified teaching churches.

The simplest illustration of the impact of technological change is that the two most effective channels for inviting strangers to visit your church in 1990 were television and direct mail. In 1999 the top two were televison and your web site. In 2003 the top two will be the Internet and television. (It is worth noting here that in early 1999 over 50 percent of all

36

households in the United States owned a personal computer, compared to only 27 percent in 1995.)

An eighth, and probably the most controversial, reason for advocating the emergence of more very large churches is the product of (a) the breakdown of the traditional family structure, the disappearance of the geographically defined neighborhood as a major force in building a sense of community; (b) the excessive expectations placed on the public schools to serve as a surrogate parent; and (c) the erosion of the influence of kinship ties. Once upon a time the public school, kinfolks, neighbors, and the parish church were willing and helpful allies in helping parents rear their children.

Today the responsibilities of parenthood are more difficult and the allies are fewer and less influential. Television, motion pictures, the Internet advertisers, and peers are more influential.

Who can and will mobilize the resources required to fulfill the promise, "We're here to help you rear your children"? Making and fulfilling that promise is becoming the distinctive asset of more and more very large congregations. It also is the closest to a guaranteed strategy for a congregation to grow younger and larger.

In more precise terms, the very large church is more likely than nine out of ten congregations to be able to create and operate the Christian day school designed to transmit the gospel of Jesus plus traditional moral values and traditional standards of ethical behavior to children. In addition, a small but growing number of congregations have accepted a partnership role with the expanding number of home-schooling families. (The big unknown at this writing is whether support for tax-supported charter schools will be confined largely to black Protestant churches and Roman Catholic parishes or whether Anglo Protestant congregations will be active allies in the charter school movement.)

Overlapping that is a ninth reason, which emerged in the later 1990s. This is the rapidly growing recognition of the contributions faith communities can make in the reduction of crime, in welfare reform, in the economic redevelopment of communities, in housing, in education, in strengthening the family structure, in reducing the divorce rate, in sheltering the homeless, in feeding the hungry, and in reducing the number of unwed teenage parents.

The United States Congress, state and local governments, foundations, corporations, and a variety of nongovernment agencies now welcome faith communities as partners in an expanding variety of social welfare endeavors. They are especially interested in faith communities with a surplus of volunteers, creativity, energy, building space, and, most in demand of all, a surplus of managerial capabilities.

The very large congregations are more likely to be able to mobilize the resources required to create new partnerships and/or to incorporate 501(c)3 nonprofit corporations than are small and midsize churches.

Finally, while far from the most exciting reason on this list, a tenth argument in support of more very large churches is ecumenism. During the 1948–90 era, denominations emerged as the basic institutional building block in the ecumenical movement. That pattern was challenged in the 1960s as a variety of congregations or movements and pastors became more involved in ecumenism. For a variety of reasons, including the increased competition for resources, by the early 1990s, two other players became more visible on the ecumenical scene. One was the coalition of senior pastors of very large congregations and megachurches. The other was and is the cooperative movements created, owned, and operated by three to fifteen very large congregations.

TWO OTHER PERSPECTIVES

Those readers who are (a) open to a highly pragmatic approach and/or (b) not threatened by a "customer-driven" or "consumer" perspective should consider two other arguments that support the contention that there is a need to at least double the number of very large Protestant congregations in the United States.

The first of these can be summarized in six words: That is what the people prefer.

Where Do People Worship?

In the 1970s and early 1980s the typical hardware store required 6,000 to 20,000 square feet of floor space, and the typical grocery supermarket covered approximately 20,000 to 30,000 square feet. Today's hardware and home supply stores require 100,000 to 140,000 square feet of floor space, and supermarkets need 60,000 to 100,000 square feet. The definition of "big" has doubled or tripled or quadrupled in a quarter of a century.

What is the definition of a very large Protestant congregation? How big does a congregation have to be to qualify as a "megachurch"?

One answer is that it depends on the denominational affiliation. If the term "megachurch" is restricted to the largest one percent of the congregations, then an average worship attendance of 500 qualifies a United Church of Christ congregation for that designation, while 675 is the cutoff point in the Evangelical Lutheran Church in America, and 625 average attendance makes it a megachurch in The United Methodist Church. At the other end of the denominational spectrum, an average worship attendance of 1,300 is required to rank among the largest one percentile in the Evangelical Free Church in America, 1,200 in the Baptist Church General Conference, 1,000 in the Reformed Church in America, 1,000 in the Assemblies of God, and 900 in the Southern Baptist Convention, the Lutheran Church-Missouri Synod, and the Wisconsin Evangelical Lutheran Synod.

39

These variations in denominational reference points can be illustrated by looking at three different systems. In the Asssemblies of God, 1.6 percent of the approximately 12,000 congregations report an average worship attendance of 800 or more. The combined average attendance of these 190 congregations in 1994 was 273,000, or approximately 18 percent of the combined attendance of all the congregations in that denomination. Those proportions are consistent with what would be expected in a large church system. At the other end of the size spectrum, the 5,200 Assemblies congregations (43 percent of all congregations) reporting an average attendance of fewer than 80 also reported a combined total of 273,000, the same as the combined total for the largest 1.6 percent in that denomination.

The Evangelical Lutheran Church in America, with nearly 11,000 congregations, is more oriented toward broadly defined middle-sized parishes, those averaging betweeen 75 and 500 at worship. Slightly under 100, or 0.9 percent, of all ELCA parishes report an average worship attendance of 800 or more. Their combined attendance of slightly over 90,000 was equivalent to nearly 6 percent of the combined worship attendance of all ELCA parishes on the typical weekend in 1995. The 2,540 smallest ELCA parishes (those averaging fewer than 55 at worship, or 23 percent of all congregations) also reported a combined worship attendance of 90,000 on the typical weekend.

A third example is The United Methodist Church, which in recent decades has been drifting in the direction of becoming a predominantly small-church denomination. By the end of 1998 only 0.5 percent of the 36,000 congregations reported an average worship attendance of 800 or more. Their combined attendance of approximately 235,000 was equivalent to 7 percent of the total worship attendance for all the churches in that denomination on the typical weekend. By contrast, the 11,600 smallest UM congregations, those averaging fewer than 40 at worship (32 percent of all UM churches), also reported a combined average worship attendance of 235,000.

A disproportionately large number of independent or non-denominational congregations have been founded since 1960 in the large central cities or in growing suburban communities, so it is not surprising to find that a disproportionately large number of very large congregations do not carry a denominational affiliation.

More significant than denominational variations, however, are geographical differences. For obvious reasons, few very large Protestant congregations are to be found in sparsely populated rural and small-town communities. They tend to be most numerous in growing metropolitan areas and especially in suburban communities that have experienced a three- to tenfold increase in population since 1960 or are on the outer edge of large metropolitan areas.

A census of churches in the metropolitan Minneapolis/St. Paul area in 1998 identified 74 Protestant and 32 Roman Catholic congregations that reported an average worship attendance of 1,000 or more. Since the number of Protestant congregations averaging 800 to 999 at worship is approximately the same as the number averaging 1,000 or more, this sugggests that there are approximately 150 Protestant churches in the Twin Cities metropolitan area that qualify as very large congregations.

In dozens of other suburban communities, somewhere between 5 and 10 percent of all Protestant churches report an average worship attendance of 800 or more. It is not uncommon, for example, for a suburban community that includes sixty Protestant congregations to report that six or seven average 800 or more at worship and that they include close to one-half of all Protestant worshipers in the typical week. The remaining 90 percent of the Protestant churches account for the remaining 50 percent of the worshipers every week.

For a variety of reasons, including demographic patterns,

41

the location of new missions, the concentration of evangelical Protestant bodies, the culture of the theological seminaries, and the differences in denominational priorities, the very large congregations tend to be located in disproportionately large numbers in the Southeast, the Southwest, southern California, Minnesota, and the south-central states. They represent a smaller proportion of all churches in the Northeast, the Midwest, the Great Plains, and the Pacific Northwest. They also were more numerous in New York, Pennsylvania, Ohio, Illinois, Iowa, and Kansas in the 1950s than they are today.

A different set of criteria surfaces if one begins by looking at the 300,000-plus worshiping communities called American Protestantism. Approximately one-half (maybe 60 percent?) report an average worship attendance of 75 or fewer, and one out of four report an average of 45 or less. Only one out of four report an average worship attendance above that "comfort zone" of 120 to 140. That size appeals to many as ideal. A church of that size usually can afford, justify, attract, challenge, and retain a fully credentialed and full-time resident pastor. It includes sufficient volunteers to staff the required offices and volunteer slots. It is able to maintain an attractive meeting place; it can avoid excessive complexity; it is able to minimize the anonymity that goes with size; nearly everyone can feel a close one-to-one relationship with the pastor; and the financial contributions from the members usually are sufficient to pay all the bills.

More important to many, however, those churches are able to both identify themselves as a congregation of X number of families or households and to come close to living out that self-image in practice. The most common illustration of that is that the schedule includes only one worship service on Sunday morning. By contrast, most very large congregations affirm the fact that they are a congregation of congregations of groups, classes, choirs, cells, circles, social networks, task forces, organizations, and fellowships.

This book is about another part of God's creation we are describing as "the very large church." These are the congregations that average 750 to 800 or more at worship over the weekend. Together they account for only 2 percent of all Protestant churches in the United States. For every very large Protestant congregation in America, there are at least 45 (exclusive of house churches) that report an average worship attendance of 350 or fewer.

Why?

If fewer than 2 percent of all the congregations in American Protestantism average 800 or more at worship, why devote a book to such a small slice of the total eccclesiastical scene?

The obvious answer is, That is where the people are. Instead of counting churches, change the subject and focus first on churchgoers. In 1998, 1 percent of all Protestant congregations in the United States accounted for 12 percent of all worshipers on the typical weekend. The largest 2 percent accounted for 17 percent, or one out of six worshipers. By contrast, the smallest 60 percent accounted for only 22 percent of all worshipers.

In 1998, 1 percent of all Protestant congregations in the United States accounted for 12 percent of all worshipers on the typical weekend. The largest 2 percent accounted for 17 percent, or one out of six worshipers. By contrast, the smallest 60 percent accounted for only 22 percent of all worshipers.

The congregations averaging 350 or more at worship account for only 5-6 percent of all Protestant churches, but they include one-third of all worshipers on the typical weekend.

In summary, three factual statements provide the justification for cutting down innocent trees simply to publish another book.

First, to meet this growing demand means either (a) the leaders in most existing congregations must be prepared to initiate significant changes in both culture and practices if they expect to become very large churches or (b) more new missions designed to become very large churches must be planted.

Second, when they perceive that they have a choice, churchgoers in disproportionately large numbers are choosing very large churches. This pattern is most visible among the churchgoers born after 1960. (It is assumed here that in the year 2035 Americans born after 1960 will greatly outnumber those born before 1940. Therefore, this is an important issue for the institutional survival of many denominational systems as well as for congregational leaders.)

As was pointed out earlier, one of the most significant ecclesiastical trends of the twentieth century has been the tripling in the average (mean) size of a Christian congregation in the United States. While an average worship attendance of 25 to 75 was the normative size for a Protestant congregation in America at the beginning of the twentieth century, that no longer is a viable size in most communities.

While the database is less than ideal, the number of very large congregations has at least tripled since 1950. In 1950, for example, the Southern Baptist Convention reported 1,019 congregations with 1,000 or more members. By 1997, that number had tripled to 3,036. Several denominations in the 1990s reported (1) an increase in the number of very large congregations and (2) a decrease in the number averaging 100 to 200 at worship. The biggest increase in the number of very large congregations has been among the independent or nondenominational churches. While the historical data are less than complete, it appears that the number of independent congregations averaging 800 or more at worship increased at least tenfold between 1960 and 2000 and probably was closer to twentyfold. The second biggest increase was among the newer and smaller denominations, such as the Baptist General Conference, the Assemblies of God, the Christian and Missionary Alliance, the Conservative Baptist Association, the Evangelical Free Church, the Evangelical Presbyterian Church, and others.

By contrast, the Methodist Church, which has a long history of running counter to contemporary American Protestantism, included 1,873 congregations reporting 1,000 or more members in 1964. Six years later, a total of 1,771 United Methodist congregations claimed 1,000 or more members, but in 1995 that number had plummeted to only 1,200.

Third—and this is a central theme of this book—if the demand is there for more very large congregations, why are there so few? Out of every 100 congregations in American Protestantism reporting an average worship attendance of 350 or more, approximately eight average 1,000 or more, another nine average 800 to 999, thirty average 500 to 799, and fifty-three average 350 to 499. Why do so few cross that 800 barrier?

A reasonable estimate is that at least one-half of those averaging 350 to 799 at worship are located in communities where (a) demographic trends indicate a doubling or tripling or quadrupling in size should be an attainable goal, (b) several relatively new congregations now average 800 or more at worship, and (c) at least a few of what once were large congregations founded before 1960 have shrunk in size.

Is it reasonable to expect that out of every 100 congregations averaging 350 or more at worship, at least 35, rather than 17, could average at least 800 at worship?

45

That is a reasonable goal, if the leaders in those large churches (a) understand and accept the fact that this probably will mean substantial changes in the culture of that congregation, (2) are able and willing to initiate the changes required for that congregation to "act like a megachurch," and (c) are willing to pay the price required to change the culture and to replace obsolete practices with "acting like a big church."

> **✝**
>
> Is it reasonable to expect that out of every 100 congregations averaging 350 or more at worship, at least 35, rather than 17, could average at least 800 at worship?

HOW BIG IS BIG ENOUGH?

In the early 1950s the typical "starter" home, the first single-family house purchased by a couple ready to become home-owners, covered approximately 800 square feet of floor space. By 1970 the average new starter home comprised 1,200 square feet. In 1998 that average new single-family home had expanded to 1,800 square feet and four out of five of all new single-family homes included central heat and air-conditioning.

People began to ask, "How high can you go in pricing new houses and still call them starter homes? There is a ceiling on what a family can afford to pay for that first house!"

A parallel set of questions is being raised today. One, which was discussed earlier, is, How large does a congregation have to be to qualify as a megachurch? If the answer is to be larger than 99 percent of the congregations in your denomination, then that requires an average worship attendance of somewhere between 500 and 1,300, depending on the culture of that denominational family.

A different question is, What is the minimum size to be able to earn a reputation for (a) relevance in preaching, worship, and learning; (b) excellence in all aspects of congregational life; and (c) the capability to offer people a range of meaningful choices in worship, learning, the group life, involvement in doing ministry, and spiritual growth?

This observer's experience suggests that the answer to that question is, At least 800 in worship in the average week.

Many senior pastors disagree and contend that the answer is at least in the 1,800 to 3,000 range. Leith Anderson, the senior pastor of Wooddale Church in suburban Minneapolis, suggests that congregations averaging 1,000 to 3,000 at worship will be able to meet the expectations of most parishioners.[7]

A different beginning point for this discussion is to raise a question that some feel should not be on the agenda. This question is based on two facts of contemporary church life. First, the replacement of the neighborhood parish by the regional church, the erosion of denominational loyalties, the decline in the power of kinship ties, and the growth of consumerism have made it relatively easy for many Christians to switch their allegiance from one religious tradition to another. Second, an increasing proportion of newcomers to the community, discontented church members, and persons on a self-identified spiritual pilgrimage frequently "shop" several congregations in their search for a new church home.

The combination of these two trends means that congregations now function in a far more competitive environment than was the pattern in the 1950s or 1960s.

What is the size that enables a congregation to be competitive? The answer varies with the rule book being used. It often depends in part on (a) the location and local environment and (b) how inclusive that congregation wants to be in defining its constituency. The Anglo congregation averaging 350 at worship and located in a small Midwestern city probably can be competitive if the leaders can accept the fact that at least four-fifths of the local residents are convinced "that is not the church for me." By contrast, the congregation in the large central city that seeks to be inclusive of various cultures and at least four generations of churchgoers probably should be able to schedule at least seven to ten different worship experiences every weekend.

The best single indicator to use in evaluating whether a particular congregation is competitive is the trend line in adults joining by letter of transfer. Are those numbers going up or down? A second, which is affected by other variables, is the trend line in the number of adults joining by profession of faith or baptism. From a denominational perspective, the question is, What proportion of the people moving into that community who come from congregations affiliated with our denomination subsequently join one of our churches?

The inability to compete resulted in the closing of a thousand hospitals in the United States between 1970 and 1998, the closing of nearly three-fourths of the 125 integrated steel blast furnaces that existed in 1978, the disappearance of two-thirds of the dairy farms that existed as recently as 1980, a reduction since 1967 of more than 50 percent in the number of gasoline service stations, a 60 percent decrease in the number of hardware stores since 1976, and the closing of an average of nine Protestant churches every day.

How large do you have to be to be competitive? For dairy farms, gasoline stations, hardware stores, supermarkets, and Protestant congregations, the simple answer is, At least twice the size that was required to be competitive in the 1960s. The exception in each example is when that institution carves out a distinctive niche for itself to serve a very precisely defined constituency.

AMBIGUITY OR CERTAINTY?

What is the number-one item on that list of common characteristics shared by a majority of these very large American Protestant congregations?

Is it great preaching? Or that most of the members were born after 1955? Or a huge worship center and acres of off-street parking? Or that they were founded after 1960? Or they are located west of the Mississippi River? Or a high priority is given to missions? Or they either do not carry a denominational label or carry it very lightly? Or the current senior minister was born in 1952 or later? Or they rely on television as their main vehicle for inviting strangers? Or their emphasis on contemporary Christian music? Or their location on the conservative end of the theological spectrum? Or their use of modern electronic channels of visual communication in worship? Or the emphasis on a single theme in the sermon rather than a three-point outline? Or the reliance on a band or an orchestra, rather than a pipe organ for music in worship? Or their operation of a Christian day school? Or that at least one-third of the dollar receipts comes from nonmembers? Or the scheduling of at least two different worship experiences every week? Or the leadership of at least one long-tenured pastor since 1960? Or the meeting place is located in a suburban community where the median income of the residents is well above that of the general population of that metropolitan area? Or the average worship attendance exceeds the reported membership? Or the priorities in the allocation of scarce resources are determined by a passion for evangelism? Or most of the program staff members are specialists and few, if any, are generalists? Or average weekly expenditures average at least $30 times the average weekly worship attendance? Or the median age of the program staff is under 45 years? Or that most of the active members report their primary social network is drawn largely or entirely from people in this congregation?

49

Any one of those two dozen generalizations applies to at least one-third of today's very large congregations, and several fit two-thirds of all big churches.

From this observer's perspective, however, the number-one point of commonality is absolute clarity about the belief system. The proclamation of the Christian gospel is organized around certainty, not ambiguity.[8] The various worship experiences offered every week may vary greatly in style, but not in substance. The visitor departs convinced, "I know what they believe and teach here." Theological pluralism and large numbers of worshipers appear to be mutually exclusive goals.

... the number-one point of commonality is absolute clarity about the belief system. The proclamation of the Christian gospel is organized around certainty, not ambiguity.

One component of that belief system that tends to be overlooked is the conviction that Christianity is a high-expectation religion. That conviction is articulated in the preaching, in the teaching, in youth ministries, in the emphasis on evangelism and missions, in the requirements for full membership, in the stewardship of time and money, in the training programs for volunteers, and in planning for the future.

Overlapping that is the line of demarcation that frequently separates the numerically shrinking large congregations from the numerically growing large churches. The shrinking churches often seek to generate broad-based support for specific and attainable goals. That is an appropriate process for small and midsize congregations in which the membership is at least double the average worship attendance. In these congregations, the usual price tag on "broad-based" and "attainable" is a watered-down compromise. The goal is set so low that it more than likely becomes a ceiling rather than a challenge.

By contrast, the numerically growing large congregations that project high expectations are more likely to focus on fulfilling the potential of that worshiping community. The difference between numerical growth and numerical decline often is a consequence of whether expectations are designed to fit comfortably under a ceiling or to rise above the floor.

Three relatively rare, but often highly visible exceptions exist to these generalizations about certainty and high expectations. The first, and most conspicuous, is the very large congregation organized around the long tenure of a magnetic personality who is an unexceptionally attractive pulpiteer. Sometimes style, not substance, is the attraction, and considerable ambiguity exists in the belief system.

A second, and more common but less visible, exception is the very large congregation organized as a collection of exceptionally high-quality specialized ministries and programs. That ministry with 300 formerly married adults may include people who come from every point on the theological spectrum, but their personal needs are recognized, affirmed, and met by that group. Likewise, the participants in those weekly prayer/Bible study groups represent a broad theological band. Some believe the current preacher is theologically sound, while others would prefer a theologically more conservative approach in the sermons; but most perceive that minister to be a close personal friend, and that compensates for the theological gap. More important, meeting every week has become one of the most meaningful experiences in their lives. That mutual support group for new parents ties another constituency into that congregation. While one-third of the members may point to worship as their number-one tie to that congregation, another 40 percent lift up their involvement in a specialized ministry, and the rest place a high value on the ministries with children and youth. The relatively high level of ambiguity in the belief system is a minor consideration.

While this was more common in the 1950s than in the 1990s, a small number of very large congregations are organized around the social status of the members. "That is the church that attracts the movers and shakers in this town." That point of commonality is given a higher value that offsets the ambiguity in the belief system.

If a congregation includes two of these three variables—the long-tenured and exceptionally attractive pastor, a variety of high-quality specialized ministries, or a large number of high-status parishioners—it may be easy for it to live with considerable ambiguity in the belief system.

The central question, however, is whether the culture of your congregation is compatible with the role and responsibilities of the very large congregation. If not, can that culture be changed? Will that require replacing the old rule book with a new edition?

CHAPTER TWO

A Larger Context

What will be the face of American Christianity in the early years of the third millennium? To a substantial degree, the answer will be shaped by what happened during the last half of the twentieth century. The impact of these and other changes in the context for doing ministry is being felt by congregations of all sizes as well as by denominational agencies and parachurch organizations. Many of these changes have created the need to revise the old rule books on how to do church in the United States. This point can be illustrated by looking briefly at a few of the most influential changes in that larger context.[1]

THE MAINLINE DECLINE

Perhaps the most widely analyzed and discussed of those changes has been the numerical decline of the mainline Protestant denominations that had dominated the American ecclesiastical scene for more than three centuries.[2] In 1906, the predecessor denominations of what today are eight mainline denominations accounted for well over one-third of all church members in the United States. Today they include fewer than one-sixth of all church members. The market share of the mainline denominations has shrunk from nearly 40 percent in 1906 to less than 16 percent in 1999.

THE ROMAN CATHOLIC MIGRATION

A second widely discussed trend was the exodus of millions of "cradle Catholics" from the Roman Catholic Church. The database is far from perfect, but apparently somewhere between 15 and 20 million adults, many of them second-, third-, fourth-, or fifth-generation American-born Catholics, have left that religious tradition. Estimates suggest that approximately one-half are now members of Protestant congregations and the other half are sitting on the sidelines. Perhaps more significant than those numbers is the conclusion of Catholic University professor William D. Dinges that many younger Catholics perceive the Roman Catholic Church to be one denominational option among many under the broad umbrella of American Christianity.

> ✝
>
> In 1906, the predecessor denominations of what today are eight mainline denominations accounted for well over one-third of all church members in the United States. Today they include fewer than one-sixth of all church members.

THE GROWTH OF OTHER RELIGIONS

While smaller in numerical terms, a third widely discussed trend of the past five decades has been the numerical growth of a variety of non-Christian religious traditions in the United States. That list includes Islam, Buddhism, the New Age movement, the Mormons, and the Black Muslims.

WHO GOES WHERE?

"We make only two promises to the people who come here," explained the senior pastor of an independent evangelical congregation that has experienced an increase in worship attendance from 300 to over 1,700 in nine years. "We promise we won't beat up on you and that we won't bore you."

The operational translation is, "Our new rule book states that you will not be criticized because you are less than a perfect Christian, the opportunities available to you in learning and in serving as a volunteer will be challenging, not boring, and every Sunday morning we offer you a chance to be part of a carefully designed, high-energy, participatory, lively, fast-paced, and highly visual worship exerience."

In 1955 approximately 50 million Americans attended one or more Christian worship services on a typical weekend. (That figure is projected from the statistical record in those congregations that record their average annual worship attendance. Projections based on the reports of pollsters produce a higher total.)

In 1955 approximately 50 million Americans attended one or more Christian worship services on a typical weekend. . . .
Forty years later, in 1995, approximately 78 million Americans worshiped in a Christian church on the typical weekend.

Forty years later, in 1995, approximately 78 million Americans worshiped in a Christian church on the typical weekend. That increase demolishes the contention that "church attendance is down all over, so we are simply a reflection of a larger national trend."

While the database is less than comprehensive, a reasonable reconstruction of history suggests that (a) the vast majority of those 50 million worshipers on the typical weekend in 1955 were believers, (b) most of those believers had inherited their religious identification from their parents or acquired it from their spouse, and (c) the primary focus in designing ministry was the care of believers.

Forty years later, the differences among congregations were far greater—although the differences among denominational traditions had decreased. Where did those 78 million Christian worshipers on the typical weekend in 1995 go to church? A five-point spectrum can be used to define where the approximately 55 million Protestants worship on that typical weekend.

A relatively small number worship with a congregation that focuses primarily on reaching nonbelievers on a self-identified religious quest. This relatively small but growing number of Protestant congregations has designed Sunday morning to persuade searchers, pilgrims, seekers, agnostics, and others of the truth and relevance of the Christian gospel. They play by their own distinctive set of rules.

Next to them on this spectrum at the end of the 1990s are the majority of Protestant churches. They concentrate on (a) serving believers and (b) helping believers transmit the faith to their children. Most of them play by a rule book that was last revised in the 1960s.

Next to them is the third group. This consists of a smaller, but substantial, number of congregations that focus on those believers who are eager to learn more about the Christian faith. The preaching and teaching emphasize "learning something new and useful today."

The relatively small, but rapidly growing, fourth segment of congregations on this spectrum consists of those churches, most of which were founded after 1968, that have developed a high level of competence in the transformation of believers and learners into deeply committed disciples of Jesus Christ. They also depend on a rule book written for that game.

A fifth and overlapping group of churches have a two-part focus: (a) the transformation of believers into disciples and (b) providing the challenge and the appropriate training for these committed disciples to become engaged in volunteer ministries. Many of these congregations rely on two rule books—one for believers on the road to discipleship and a different edition for those who are apostles.

From this observer's perspective, it appears that the second group of churches, those that concentrate on serving believers, many of whom inherited their church affiliation from their parents or acquired it from their spouse, are seeing their members grow older in age and fewer in numbers. Together these congregations account for most of the decrease in worship attendance. That decrease has been more than offset by the increase in worshipers in the first, third, fourth, and fifth groups on that spectrum. A disproportionately large number of the congregations in the first, fourth, and fifth segments on that specrum of congregations are independent or nondenominational churches or are affiliated with one of the newer religious traditions in the United States.

This change in where Protestant worshipers go to church is one of the half dozen most significant developments of the second half of the twentieth century and has radically altered the national context for ministry. One by-product is a fifth trend.

BEYOND THE MAINSTREAM

This fifth trend is the continued growth in the numbers, the adherents, and the impact of congregations not affiliated with one of the mainline denominations. That list includes highly visible denominations such as the Southern Baptists, the Assemblies of God, the Presbyterian Church in America, the Seventh-Day Adventists, and the Evangelical Free Church of America, but it also includes movements such as the Vineyard,[3] the Churches of Christ, the American Baptist Association, and associations of congregations, such as the Conservative Baptist Association, plus thousands of completely independent and autonomous nondenominational churches. Together these congregations account for most of the net growth among Protestant churchgoers. (The two other big growth areas that have offset the numerical decline of the predominantly Anglo mainstream denominations have been [a] the organization of new immigrant churches and [b] the numerical growth of a few thousand megachurches, including scores of very large black congregations.)

THE IMPACT OF RISING EXPECTATIONS

Where do you go if you want to purchase flowers to decorate your dining room table or your living room or as a gift? In 1985 the answer was a florist shop. When you leave the medical clinic, the physician hands you a prescription for a new medication. Where do you go to have that prescription filled? In 1985, the common answer was the corner drugstore.

Today's consumer, however, prefers one-stop shopping. One result is that in 1998 more than four out of five of the 25,000 American supermarkets sold flowers, compared to one in five in 1985. A second is the increasing number of supermarkets and discount stores that also house a pharmacy. One way to serve a larger constituency is to expand the range of services offered.

A parallel trend is that many churchgoers now expect their congregation to offer all-day child care five days a week, a varied recreation program for adults as well as for children and youth, breakfast and/or a noon meal every Sunday, attractive opportunities to meet and make new friends, highly skilled help in how to rear your children, an adult day-care ministry two or three days a week, the counsel of a parish nurse, carefully organized trips to learn from that growing number of teaching churches, counsel in preparing income tax returns, after-school activities for children, the possibility of meeting one's future spouse, classes for expectant parents, a variety of

12-Step support groups, exercise classes, square dancing, language classes, a yearly visit to the Holy Land, a prekindergarten nursery school, an abundance of off-street parking, and clean, modern rest rooms.

If a grocery store chooses not to house a branch bank or not to sell cut flowers, it does not have to do that, but a competitor down the street probably will respond to that demand.

The larger and the more varied the expectations people project on the church, the greater the advantages of the large congregation that can mobilize the resources required to meet that demand.

One of the clearest examples of the impact of rising expectations can be seen on the campus of the large university. As a professor at a prestigious eastern school described it, "The place is looking more and more like a retirement center for youth."[4] The big difference between it and the retirement villages in the Sunbelt is that residents of the latter use their savings to live there, while many of today's students borrow the needed dollars.

The relevant question here, however, is, Which set of expectations will the churches have to deal with in the year 2010? Those brought by people who attended the university in the 1930s, 1940s, and 1950s? Or the far larger number who attended in the 1990s? (Many of the issues raised in this book are based on the assumption that people born in the 1970s and 1980s will outlive those born in the 1920s and 1930s.)

PEERS OR PARENTS?

One slice of this demand for help reflects a century-long debate over the influential forces in the socialization of children and youth into the American culture. One group of parents is convinced that today's teenagers are heavily influenced by their peers. (Television, motion pictures, and advertising could be added to that list.) Therefore, these parents often seek a congregation in which (a) their children will meet and make friends with peers who come from a home environment based on a compatible value system, (b) the youth ministries are designed to encourage peer leadership, and (c) the ministries with children are highly structured. If peers are so influential, these parents want their children to be socialized with peers who display the "right" set of moral values and standards of ethical behavior.

Many of these parents of younger children also seek a church that offers a weekday prekindergarten program for three year olds and four year olds, plus a Christian day school through at least grade six.

On the other side of this ideological fence are the parents who are convinced that parents, teachers, and other adults are highly influential in the socialization of children and youth. They tend to look for a church home that (a) offers a variety of parenting classes designed for various stages of the life cycle; (b) has a youth program that is largely staffed by several volunteers, each of whom is an attractive model of a deeply committed adult Christian; (c) places a greater emphasis on families than on individuals in designing ministries; and (d) welcomes teenagers to be active participants with adults in vocal and instrumental music groups, in learning experiences, in worship, in drama, and in other volunteer roles.

The peer leadership model usually calls for a person with the title "Youth Minister" or "Youth Pastor" on the program staff. In the second model, that position is more likely to be filled by a person responsible for "ministries with families that include teenagers."

Both sets of expectations exceed the available resources in most congregations averaging fewer than 350 to 500 at worship.

This distinction between peer leaders and adult leaders as a central organizing principle in youth ministries illustrates one facet of the rising expectations that younger generations are bringing to church. It also illustrates (a) the increased demands on paid staff to "meet my expectations," (b) how new ministries also can become a source of internal conflict, (c) the demand for a higher level of intentionality in designing ministry, and (d) how the continuity in ministry can be disrupted when a replacement program staff specialist arrives with a different set of assumptions, values, and goals than those held by the predecessor.

WHO PLANTED THE FUTURE CROP OF MEGACHURCHES?

Perhaps the least widely discussed, but one of the most significant, trends of the last third of the twentieth century was the decision by several mainline Protestant denominations in the 1960s and 1970s to cut back sharply on planting new congregations. The predecessor denominations of the Evangelical Lutheran Church in America together started a combined total of approximately 1,000 new missions during the 1960s. During the first decade of its existence, the new Evangelical Lutheran Church in America planted a total of 232 new missions. During the 1950s, the Methodist Church averaged nearly 200 new missions annually. That dropped to an annual average of 50 in 1966–69 and to 20 in 1970–74. The two predecessor denominations of the Presbyterian Church (U.S.A.) organized an average of well over a hundred new missions annually in the late 1950s and early 1960s, compared to an average of 57 in the 1979–88 era.[5]

This cutback in new church development by the mainline denominations created a vacuum that has been filled by the Southern Baptist Convention and several other evangelical denominations, by new movements such as the Vineyard, and by the independent nondenominational congregations.

More relevant to this discussion is the distribution of very large congregations. A reasonable estimate is that the number of Lutheran, Presbyterian, United Methodist, Christian Church (Disciples of Christ), United Church of Christ, Episcopal, Reformed Church in America, and American Baptist congregations averaging 800 or more at worship is one-half the number it would be today if that cutback in new church development had not occurred. What was not planted in the 1960s, the 1970s, and the 1980s does not bloom today.

FROM SMALL TO BIG INSTITUTIONS

Another significant societal trend was introduced earlier. That is the shift from small to big institutions all across American society. That list includes financial institutions, new car dealers, grocery stores, universities, medical clinics, motels, elementary schools, motion picture theaters, book-stores, airlines, variety stores, and churches. The generations born before 1940 grew up in, and were socialized by, small institutions. The generations born after World War II learned how to be comfortable in a world of big institutions. That also helps to explain why a majority of the worshipers in many small congregations come from the generations born before 1940, while younger generations form the majority in most very large churches.

WHOM DO WE TRUST?

The middle third of the twentieth century was a period when Americans trusted large and distant institutions. The federal government, colleges and universities, the military, political parties, denominational systems, hospitals, high schools, brand names, automobile manufacturers, and the churches were trusted to tell people what to do and how to do it. Then came 1968![6] That year marked the end of an era.

If you cannot trust the big and distant institutions to act in your best interests, what do you do? One response is simply to drop out. The proportion of the voting age population in the United States who voted in mid-term elections dropped from 48.6 percent in 1966 to 40.1 percent in 1980 to 36.1 percent in 1998. Denominational meetings and rallies no longer attract the crowds they once did. The federal government found it could not arouse the local support for new programs that marked the 1950s and 1960s (such as federally designed highways and housing programs) and shifted to block grants to states and local governments.

Another response was and is to trust individuals who have earned that trust. In the 1950s, presidents, police officers, parents, politicians, professors, pastors, priests, the pope, physicians, and others were trusted because of the office they held and/or because of their credentials. Once upon a time professors evaluated the performance of students. Today's university students expect to be asked to evalute the performance of the professors.

Another response that had some visibility in the 1930s and 1950s, but did not blossom until the 1960s, was that through collective action people who were deemed to be powerless could take collective action to change those large and distant institutions. Examples include the student rebellions of 1968, the anti-Vietnam war protest, the civil rights movement, the growing use of the voter-initiated referendum in state and local elections, the emergence of influential caucuses in denominational systems, the power of a variety of consumer groups that have generated boycotts of corporations and/or products, and rent strikes by tenants.

One consequence of this expanded reliance on collective action is an extraordinary increase in litigation. Today the threat of litigation is a powerful factor in many policy decisions on employment policies, promotions, and launching new products or programs. This threat of litigation also requires revising the old rule book.

From this observer's perspective, it is not a coincidence that this spreading distrust of large and distant institutions is related to (a) the rapid growth in the number of independent congregations in which most or all of the authority is lodged in the pastor and a small number of volunteer lay elders (if you are unhappy with a decision, you do not appeal it to a denominational agency; you either accept that decision, or you leave) and (b) the increase in the internal conflict and litigation in those religious traditions that continue to stress their role as regulatory bodies (the Roman Catholic Church, The United Methodist Church, the Presbyterian Church [U.S.A.], the Reformed Church in America, the Christian Reformed Chuch, the Southern Baptist Convention, and the Lutheran Church-Missouri Synod are examples).

The polity of two of the largest religious bodies in the United States, the Roman Catholic Church and The United Methodist Church, is based on the assumption that local leadership cannot be trusted. The recent research of Francis Fukuyama, Robert Putnam, Wendy Rahn, Eric Uslaner, Ron Inglehart, Rafael La Porta, Florencio Lopez-de-Silanes, Andrei Shleifer, Robert Vishny, and other scholars has revealed a high correlation between a low level of internal trust within an institution and low performance. Putnam and others also argue that religious systems based on vertical lines of authority, rather than horizontal lines of relationships, discourage the formation of trust.[7]

It may not be a coincidence that a characteristic of nearly all Protestant megachurches is a high level of internal trust of local leadership.

DOES IT TAKE A VILLAGE?

One of the most significant trends was identified in the opening pages of the Introduction. For most of American history, and especially in rural and small-town communities, informal but highly effective coalitions accepted most of the responsibility for socializing children into the culture of this new nation. These coalitions included the nuclear family, neighbors, kinfolk, 4-H clubs, scouting, the public schools, and the church. To a remarkable degree they shared a common set of core values, and their goals and actions were mutually reinforcing. Parents who were open to help and counsel found it to be readily available.

During the past half century, divorce and the changing demands of the labor force have undermined the cohesive nature of the family. Kinship ties are far less influential, social networks are being built on points of commonality other than the place of residence so that neighbors often are strangers or acquaintances rather than sources of help. The neighborhood church is being replaced by regional congregations. The public schools have been overwhelmed by (a) excessive expectations placed upon them to fill the role of surrogate parents and (b) a reduction in their authority to even fulfill their old role as primarily educational institutions.[8]

One result is a growing demand by parents for help in rearing their children. Many very large congregations now (a) affirm this as a legitimate expectation for parents to bring to a worshiping community; (b) have decided to be responsive to this demand; (c) have hired the staff, built their ministries, and constructed the necessary physical facilities. The worshiping community becomes the replacement for the village in helping parents rear their children.

THE IMPACT OF THE FEDERAL GOVERNMENT

Changes in the depreciation schedules for new construction sparked the construction of the regional shopping centers in the 1960s. The construction of better roads, the subsidies that encouraged the growth of suburbia, and the increased dependence on the private motor vehicle have combined to make it relatively easy for people to drive ten or twenty or thirty miles each way to church two or three or four times a week. The size of a congregation no longer is limited by the number of residents living within a mile or two of the meeting place.

THE EROSION OF INHERITED LOYALTIES

As recently as the 1950s and 1960s many adults carried loyalties inherited from their parents. These included loyalty to a particular political party, to a specific religious tradition, to a brand name in food or automobiles or retail stores, to a college or university, and to a major league sports team. The 1960s brought a new era. Institutional loyalties had to be earned; they were not automatically inherited. This has made it easier for cradle Catholics, fourth-generation Presbyterians, the adult children of Methodist preachers, and others to leave the religious tradition in which they had been reared and join that nondenominational megachurch. This change has been reinforced by the sharp increase in interfaith and interdenominational marriages.

When this trend is combined with the replacement of the neighborhood parish by the regional church, it is easy to explain why so many people switch religious traditions when they look for a new church home. They have more choices than their parents and grandparents had.

This erosion of inherited institutional loyalties coincided with a sharp decline in anti-Catholicism among American Protestants after 1962 and with the growing attractiveness of the ecumenical movement. The new slogan for ecumenism was, "Instead of emphasizing the differences that separate us, let us focus on what we have in common."

If, in an evaluation of the ecumenical movement, the focus is shifted from the relationships of religious institutions to the attitudes and behavior of people, a startling conclusion emerges. The most impressive success story of contemporary ecumenism is the migration of millions of adults out of Roman Catholic and denominationally affiliated Protestant congregations into new and rapidly growing nondenominational or independent churches. It is not at all unusual for the very large congregation to report that 25 to 40 percent of its present constituents were reared in a Catholic home and another 25 to 40 percent were born into a family affiliated with a Protestant denomination. This usually means a revision of that congregation's old rule book.

WHO KILLED THE SUNDAY SCHOOL?

"My wife and I decided we needed to visit that new nondenominational megachurch on the west side of town," explained sixty-seven-year-old Jim Baxter to five members from their Sunday school class as they enjoyed dinner together one Tuesday evening at the Baxters' home. "We agreed we needed a firsthand experience there so we could learn why they are so successful in attracting young families."

"Well, what did you learn?" inquired the guest who also was the treasurer of that adult class.

"We learned a lot," replied Jim, "but our biggest surprise was to discover they do not have a Sunday school! Their Sunday morning schedule consists of two consecutive ninety-minute worship services plus an inquirers' class for prospective future members at each hour."

"What do they do with the children?" asked another guest.

"They offer two alternatives," explained Jim. "One is a children's church service at each hour for children ages four to ten, plus a youth service, also at each hour, for those ages eleven to fourteen. The second alternative is they encourage parents to bring their children to church at each service. They also have child care for very young children at both services. We were told youth ages fourteen and above are strongly encouraged to be in worship every Sunday morning."

"Well, I find that hard to believe!" commented another. "I can't imagine a church without a Sunday school, especially one that is designed to reach young families. My guess is the next five years will see a substantial shrinkage in their size."

"Maybe not," challenged that guest's husband. "They may be appealing to an audience who wants church every week, but doesn't want too much church. Sounds to me like you can go there on Sunday morning and be back home within two hours. That will appeal to a lot of people. Betty and I usually leave the house about ten after nine on Sunday morning to be on time for our nine-thirty adult class, and we go to the eleven o'clock service. We seldom get home before twelve-twenty to twelve-forty. That is an investment of more than three hours. I can believe there are a lot of young people who would prefer to limit that to two hours."

"Don't they have any instruction for their chilren?" asked Esther Hoyt, a widowed grandmother.

"We checked that out," explained Jim, "and we were told that they have a big Wednesday afternoon and evening educational program. The children and youth come directly to the church from school. That gives them about two hours for religious instruction. That is followed by a meal, to which all adults also are invited, followed by a variety of adult classes, the weekly meeting of three different youth fellowships for three different age groups, rehearsal time for about a dozen different music groups, and crafts and other activities for children. We were told the combined attendance for the two services on Sunday morning is close to 1,400, including the kids in children's church, and that Wednesday evening runs nearly 1,000."

"That makes our hour-long Sunday school with an average attendance under 200 look kind of feeble by comparison," reflected the treasurer.

This account illustrates four contemporary trends. One is the emergence of scores of relatively new nondenominational megachurches. A second is that the larger the size of the crowd, the more likely the worship service will be closer to 75 to 90 minutes in length rather than an hour. A third is the renewed interest in children's church. A fourth is the gradual disappearance of the traditional hour-long Sunday school for children.

WHAT HAPPENED?

In a growing number of Protestant congregations the time for the religious instruction of children has been moved out of Sunday morning. One alternative is the Christian day school. A second is after school one afternoon every week. A third, and far less common, is after school on two or three or four or five afternoons every week. After-school child care and religious instruction are combined, partly for the benefit of parents employed outside the home. A fourth alternative is to move it to a Saturday morning. A fifth, which is just over the horizon, will be the charter school meeting in a church building that offers religious instruction before the beginning and/or after the end of the school day.

> In a growing number of Protestant congregations the time for the religious instruction of children has been moved out of Sunday morning.

WHY?

Among the many reasons for this displacement of the traditional children's Sunday school, a dozen are frequently cited.

1. A session of 45 to 60 minutes is not sufficient time to accomplish what needs to be done in the teaching ministries.

2. Many congregations are actively encouraging parents to participate with their children in the corporate worship of God.

3. The biblical illiteracy of today's younger adults suggests that the Sunday school classes of twenty years ago were not effective learning experiences.

4. It is easier to enlist teachers for Wednesday after school or Saturday morning than for Sunday morning.

5. The top priority for Sunday morning is to offer people a choice between two attractive, but different, worship experiences. Scheduling Sunday school for Sunday morning overloads the schedule.

6. The demand by adults for meaningful learning experiences creates a need for 120- to 150-minute classes that cannot be squeezed into Sunday morning, so why not move most of the teaching ministries to one evening?

7. With the meal at the middle of the Wednesday evening program, new possibilities to focus on the nuclear family unit as the number-one constituency open up.

8. That Wednesday evening schedule opens the door for teaching by the pastor and other program staff members.

9. Scheduling two "peak hour" times during the week, rather than attempting to squeeze everything into Sunday morning, allows us to make more efficient use of our limited space.

10. That big Wednesday program provides several attractive entry points for potential future members.

11. With the growing competition for people's time on Sunday, that four- to five-hour block of time on Wednesday provides a more relaxed and pressure-free time for learning and fellowship.

12. The parents want more for their children than we can offer in a 45- to 60-minute period on Sunday morning.

One consequence is the continued shrinkage in the number of congregations offering the traditional Wednesday evening prayer meeting. Another is the need to revise the rule book to accommodate this new emphasis on learning.

A third consequence is the increase in the level of competition among the churches to determine which one offers the most attractive alternative to the traditional Sunday morning children's Sunday school.

FROM LAW TO GRACE

From this observer's perspective, one of the half dozen most influential changes is represented by many of the adult children of members of the fundamentalist congregations of the 1950s. Many of these churches were organized around Holy Scripture as the sole source of authority and guidance. They proclaimed a highly legalistic interpretation of the Bible that also emphasized punishment for misbehavior. Law, not grace, was the central theme of most of the preaching and teaching. Among the clearly identifiable enemies were the humanities, the behavioral sciences, and higher criticism.[9]

Forty years later, where are the children and grandchildren of the members of those fundamentalist churches of the 1950s? A substantial number, including many senior pastors of today's very large churches, can be found in what now are identified as evangelical congregations. Typically they affirm Scripture as the central source of authority but are open to insights and learnings from the behavioral sciences in designing new ministries. Forgiveness receives far more emphasis than is given to eternal damnation in both the preaching and the teaching. They also use a radically different rule book on how to do church in today's world.

WILL AMERICANIZATION WORK?

The jury is still out on what may turn out to be one of the most crucial components of the societal context for ministry.

71

Will the churches be effective agents in facilitating the integration into American society of recent immigrants from other parts of the world?

The Census of Religious Bodies conducted by the United States Bureau of the Census in 1906 reported that in 1906 more than four out of five Lutheran church members belonged to congregations that scheduled weekly worship in a language other than English. These Lutheran parishes served as a bridge between the members' ties to "the old country" and to America. Recent ancestry studies from the 1980 and 1990 censuses suggest that by the third and fourth generations, the descendants of Western European immigrants were well assimilated into American society. The public schools, employers, the churches, and local governments were among the most effective forces in facilitating that assimilation. Intermarriage across nationality lines became very high with the third generation.[10]

The big unknown today is whether the churches will encourage assimilation or ethnic, nationality, language, and racial separation. The big difference between today and ninety years ago is that in 1906 most Christian churches in the United States carried a Western European heritage. That made it relatively easy to assimilate second-, third-, and fourth-generation newcomers. Today the "Made in America" religious traditions constitute a much larger proportion of Protestantism, and the vast majority of recent immigrants are not coming from Western Europe.

THE RISE OF UNBELIEF

What if the report by the independent special prosecutor Kenneth Starr had been released in 1958 rather than in 1998?

First of all, that investigation probably would not have taken place. Second, if it had, the language in the report almost certainly would have been far less specific! Third, it is doubtful whether the newspapers would have printed every word in every sentence. The belief system, the moral values, the standards of ethical behavior, and the doctrines proclaimed by the Christian churches created a climate for public discourse far different from what existed in 1998. The old rule book of 1958 has been replaced by a revised edition!

The middle third of the twentieth century marked the beginning of the end of a centuries-long era in which the existence of God was an accepted fact of life among both white and black Americans. Up until the 1850s, disbelief was not widely perceived as an option. Gradually, however, disbelief began to become an acceptable alternative; but it was not until the 1950s and 1960s that it became a respectable option for intellectuals and molders of public opinion.

In the 1950s those who chose the alternative of unbelief were still on the defensive. Forty years later believers often found themselves on the defensive. This can be seen most clearly in the criteria used to define acceptable language, appropriate behavior, the choice of moral values to be transmitted to the next generation, the definition of the standards of ethical behavior, what is off-limits in public schools, the standards for evaluating the conduct of public officials, and the qualifications required to be employed as a teacher in a church-related college, university, or theological school.

The contemporary acceptance of unbelief has changed the context for doing ministry as much as any other trend described in this book.

THE BIG UNKNOWN

In 1969 women held 4 percent of all the seats in the legislatures of the fifty states. Ten years later that proportion had risen to 10.3 percent. In 1993 it had climbed to 20.5 percent, and in 1999 it was 22.3 percent. In 1999 Washington State ranked at the top of that list with 40.8 percent of all legislative seats filled by women, and women outnumbered men on the Democratic side of the state senate by an 18 to 9 ratio. In Nevada, Arizona, Colorado, and Kansas, women acccounted for approximately one-third of the state legislators in 1999.

The last third of the twentieth century saw a rapid increase in the proportion of women among dentists, lawyers, physicians, bus drivers, university professors, accountants, mayors, planners, parish pastors, college presidents, television anchorpersons, newspaper reporters, hospital administrators, and other vocations.

What will be the proportion of women among parish pastors in the year 2050? Will it be 30 percent? 40 percent? 60 percent? Are women more likely to be serving as pastors of small to middle-sized congregations that place a premium on relational skills?[11] Or as senior ministers of large and very large congregations? Does this mean that a major revision of the rule book is overdue?

As we begin the twenty-first century, this is an unknown factor. But it could become a highly influential variable in predicting the future of the megachurch in America.

LIBERAL TO CONSERVATIVE

While this last observation probably should not be offered before the year 2050, it now appears that the twentieth century can be divided into three parts. The first third was controlled by the conservatives. The second third (1933–68) was clearly a liberal era. During the last third, the pendulum swung back to a more conservative climate. This can be seen in the arena of partisan politics; in the redefinition of the role of the federal government; in the design of social welfare programs; in the administration of the criminal justice system; in that remarkable increase in the number of adults engaged in serious and in-depth Bible study groups for two to two and one-half hours every week; in American foreign policy; in the effort to produce a balanced federal budget; in the numerical growth of the theologically more conservative Protestant congregations; in the criteria used to select bishops, archbishops, and cardinals in the American Catholic Church; in the decline in the influence of the National Council of the Churches of Christ; in the huge contemporary market for books on spirituality; and in the climate for entrepreneurship.

This raises a crucial question: Will the early years of the new millennium be marked by a continuation of a national conservative climate? Or will the pendulum swing back toward liberalism? Will the liberals and the conservatives of the year 2010 be able to play by the same rule book?

At this point a few bored readers may interrupt, "You have neglected the most significant change of all in that larger context!" They may be right, but that one deserves a chapter by itself.

CHAPTER THREE

The Consequences of Consumerism

O ne of the most significant watersheds in the history of American higher education followed the inaugura- tion of Charles William Eliot as president of Harvard in 1869. In the 1870s, Harvard pioneered the elective system, which allowed students to choose many of their courses. In 1885, in a debate with the president of Princeton, Eliot declared that a university "must try to teach every subject . . . for which there is any demand."[1]

Eighty years after that famous debate, hundreds of colleges and universities had sharply reduced the number of required courses in the core curriculum to enable students to customize their schedules to fit their own self-identified needs.

It was not until the 1998–99 academic year, however, that the University of Chicago decided to reduce its required core curriculum for first- and second-year undergraduates from twenty-one courses to eighteen, effective in September 1999. This was one component of a larger strategy to make the uni- versity more attractive to potential applicants. Despite an earned reputation as one of the world's great intellectual cen- ters, the undergraduate program attracts only one-half to one-third as many applicants as other topflight schools, such as Stanford and Princeton. In this era of a consumer-driven approach to higher education, the University of Chicago also plans to spend $35 million to construct a new student center and swimming pool, to improve career placement services, and to increase the number of student clubs. Consumerism has come to the most elite of American institutions!

The Consequences of Consumerism

From a long-term historical perspective, the greatest impact of consumerism for Americans came in the last third of the eighteenth century. That was when the colonists came out in opposition to taxation without representation and eventually went to war with England over that issue.

For several generations it was widely assumed that a basic responsibility of every Protestant denomination in the United States was to create, publish, and market a hymnal that undergirded the theological and doctrinal position of that religious tradition. These thick, heavy, clothbound books usually (a) made money for that denominational publishing house and (b) were followed by a revised edition every twenty to fifty years. Congregations were expected to sing the hymns chosen by the elite committee that produced the new hymnal. (In early 1998, one-third of the pastors surveyed in the Presbyterian Church [U.S.A.] reported their congregations never use the denominational hymnal in worship.)

Desktop publishing came along in the 1980s and, combined with new simplified licensing procedures for copyrighted materials, made it both easy and economical for any congregation to publish its own hymnal. A typical process calls for a task force to encourage members to submit the names of their favorite hymns.

The members of the task force may expand that list, and each member may be asked to choose the hymns that must be included. The hundred that receive the most votes are chosen. Fees are paid for licensing, a copy machine is used to reproduce the text and music for each one, a cover is designed and printed. Within a few weeks the new paperbound hymnal is available at a modest cost per copy. (A few congregations have bound a picture directory of the members into their personalized hymnal.)

The consumers have replaced the producers in choosing the hymns a congregation will sing. The critics contend that means placing in charge the people who know the least about classical Christian music and that particular denomination's history, doctrine, and traditions.

These examples illustrate two trends that are redefining the larger context for ministry. One is the growth of consumerism. A second is the erosion of the power of the producers of goods and services. That has produced a predictable reaction by the producers who object to a loss of control. One example that will have a huge impact on the early years of the twenty-first century is in the decentralization of higher education. The producers, university faculty in particular, want students to come to them. The consumers, especially those past age twenty-two, want the professors to come to them. The producers also are losing power to the consumers in the delivery of health-care services, in the design of television programs, in the scheduling of major league baseball play-off games and the World Series, in the design of retail facilities (as the "big one-story boxes" compete with the two- or three-story enclosed shopping malls), and in the publishing business.

The consumers have replaced the producers in choosing the hymns a congregation will sing. The critics contend that means placing in charge the people who know the least about classical Christian music and that particular denomination's history, doctrine, and traditions.

For many, the big shock came with the gradual recognition that this means a change in the role and responsibilities of producers. One example of this is the dramatic change in assumptions about listening. In the 1950s it was widely assumed that the 300 students who came to that lecture given by the university professor in that huge hall brought with them an obligation to listen intently, absorb, take notes, and learn. The professor might be repeating a dull lecture given twenty times before, but the students were expected to listen and learn. Likewise, it was assumed that when worshipers came to church, they bore the responsibility to listen carefully to the sermon.

Forty years of television have taught younger generations that the producers of lectures, sermons, and other forms of oral communication carry 100 percent of the responsibility for grabbing and holding the attention of the potential listener.

Forty years of television have taught younger generations that the producers of lectures, sermons, and other forms of oral communication carry 100 percent of the responsibility for grabbing and holding the attention of the potential listener.

The impact of this shift in responsibility already has caused the thousands of high school teachers to (1) master new pedagogical skills or (2) retire early or (3) choose a different vocation or (4) complain. The impact also is beginning to be felt by college and university teachers. The clearest evidence of this trend can be seen in the criteria used by undergraduates to evaluate professor performance in the major research universities.[2]

CONSUMERS WANT ENTERTAINMENT!

This has led to what many critics identify as the most unfortunate consequence of consumerism.[3] Restaurants once were evaluated on the basis of the quality of the food and service. In recent years ambience and entertainment have been added to that list of criteria. The shopping mall is expected to be an entertainment center. The newer ones may include a roller coaster, an IMAX theater, and a variety of virtual reality games. The shopping trip today often includes high-tech entertainment. "Entertaining speaker" now ranks above "scholar" among the criteria used by the program committee in choosing a platform speaker for a big event. The anchor team presenting the evening news on the local television station often includes four people—a man and a woman, one of whom represents an ethnic minority group, plus a sports reporter and a meteorologist. The last two often are expected to double as entertainers.

An ever-growing proportion of the population wants to be informed and entertained concurrently, and they believe that these are compatible expectations. Museums, producers of the news on network television, advertising agencies, the weekly newsmagazines such as *Time* and *Newsweek*, high school science teachers, television, newsmagazines, preachers, candidates for election to public office, Disney, and many of the contemporary "seeker-sensitive" churches are examples of combining entertainment and information.

Entertainment has emerged as an industry in itself. National newspapers, such as the *New York Times* and the *Wall Street Journal*, have added whole sections devoted to entertainment. Disney contends that its secret of success is in combining information and entertainment. A common compliment heard by professors, preachers, and lecturers is, "I really enjoyed what you had to say."

The Internet may turn out to be the most influential force in increasing the power of consumerism and eroding the role of the producers of goods and services.

The Internet offers consumers two-way communication, a vast range of choices, anonymity, economy, freedom from geographical limitations, visual communication, a huge reservoir of easily accessible information, 24-hour-a-day shopping, and unlimited sources of entertainment.

Before looking at some of the consequences of consumerism for the churches, it may be useful to look at the larger scene. Where has the impact been the greatest?

WHO HAS BEEN AFFECTED?

A list of those most affected by consumerism includes retailers such as grocery, drug, variety, and hardware stores; gasoline stations; hospitals; radio stations; newspapers; magazines; and institutions of higher education, including theological schools. The design and sale of motor vehicles also have been shaped by the demands of consumers.

Perhaps the greatest recent impact, however, has been on the motel industry. As recently as 1961 the number of motel establishments exceeded 61,000, many of which were owned and operated by an American-born husband-wife couple. By 1987, the number of establishments had dropped to fewer than 40,000, but the number of rooms had quadrupled to over 3 million in 1994.

During the last third of the twentieth century, it became clear to the motel industry that the customer wanted privacy; a convenient parking space; a clean room; safety; predictability; a segmented market in terms of price, space, quality, and extras; and a customer-friendly reservation system. Motel chains and franchised operations have largely replaced the "Mom and Pop" motels of the 1930–60 era.[4] Motels also are now providing employment opportunities for adults born in Southeast Asia and Latin America.

One lesson for the churches from the transformation of the motel industry can be stated very simply: When the traveler stopped at the "Mom and Pop" motel, both parties usually assumed that the traveler could and should examine the available room before registering. Today the traveler stops at the brand-name motel and assumes that a guest room will be acceptable and does not need to be inspected before registering.

The parallel is the newcomer to the community used to worshiping with three to a dozen or more different congregations before choosing a new church home. Today a growing number of these newcomers immediately go to a very large congregation with the expectation that this will become their new church home. That expectation may be based on the national reputation of that church, on the recommendation of their pastor back home, on that congregation's web site, or on an earlier visit to what also is a regional or teaching church. "Shopping" for a motel room is far less common today than it was in the 1970s or 1980s. Will the increase in the number of very large congregations reduce the number of church shoppers? Or will consumerism lead people to rely on two or three congregations every week to meet their religious needs, just as they now purchase their groceries from two or three different supermarkets?

One of the most significant consequences of consumerism in the business world is reflected in the growing number of corporations that have restructured themselves. Originally their corporate structure was designed to focus on their producer role or their products. One division might focus on laundry detergents, another would concentrate on kitchen cleansers, a third on bathroom supplies, a fourth would be responsible for sales, and a fifth would specialize in advertising. The new structure is designed around clusters of consumers such as one-person households, commercial users, families with children at home, and first-time parents.

The congregational counterpart to this trend can be seen in newspaper advertising. As recently as the 1980s many congregations still purchased a weekly newspaper ad, which reflected a producer perspective. It carried the name, address, and telephone number of that congregation plus the weekend schedule for worship and Sunday school. A few also listed the sermon title and text plus the name of the preacher.

The arrival of the consumer era changed that. Some churches simply dropped the newspaper ad from their annual budget because of ineffectiveness. Others headlined a question, "Need help raising your children?" "Looking for answers to your spiritual questions?" "Are you a newlywed?" "Searching for a church home?" "Do you want more out of church than a short nap?" That question was followed by a brief statement exlaining how that congregation could meet your need.

The regional denominational judicatory was organized around the specialties of the staff, such as camping, Christian education, evangelism, stewardship, missions, and worship. The replacement structure is organized around the needs of congregations, including counseling with small congregations, designing worship experiences for people born after 1965, planning a capital funds campaign, advice on relocation of the meeting place, and planting new missions.

In theological education the shift is from an organizational structure reflecting various academic disciplines to one that addresses what the graduates will be doing in the parish ministry. (See item 21 in chapter 9.)

Among the institutions least influenced by consumerism are public elementary schools, the large commercial airlines (except for Southwest Airlines, which is a consumer favorite that has been able to substitute economy and entertainment for food), monopolies such as the Postal Service and utilities (both of which began to feel the impact of consumerism in the late 1990s), denominational systems, and at least 60 percent of all Protestant congregations.

The most surprising consequence of consumerism came in 1998 when Congress adopted legislation ordering the Internal Revenue Service to become more customer friendly.

A HERITAGE FROM THE 1960s

The increasing concern about the impact of consumerism began to surface in the 1980s, but that simply represented the normal institutional lag between the emergence of a change in the culture and the public recognition of the change. Consumerism is a natural product of the American emphasis on freedom. Most of the readers of this volume are the descendants of people who left another continent to come to North America in their consumer-driven quest for religious, political, or economic freedom. Consumerism and that same desire for greater individual freedom is what motivated most of the recent immigrants to come to North America. The economic affluence of the American population during the last third of the twentieth century opened the doors wider for the growth of consumerism.

A persuasive argument can be made that in symbolic terms the current wave of consumerism in the United States traces back to a statement adopted by sixty college students in 1962. This was the famous Port Huron Statement of Students for a Democratic Society (SDS), originally drafted by Tom Hayden.[5] Most of the statement focused on criticism of the institutions of American life, ranging from corporations and trade unions to military organizations. In 1962 it was widely perceived as a radical critique from the revolutionary left. A few sentences, however, are now widely accepted under the umbrella of consumer rights. These include the plea for people to have a voice in the decisions that will affect their lives and a brief for "participatory democracy." One famous sentence reads, "As a social system we seek the establishment of a democracy of individual participation, governed by two central aims: that the individual share in those social decisions determining the quality and direction of his life; that society be organized to encourage independence in men and provide the media for their common participation."[6] The Statement goes on to demand that work be designed to be educative, creative, and self-directed and to encourage independence, respect for the dignity of others, and social responsibility, not simply as a way to make money.

84

The next four decades brought many changes in the American economic, political, and social climate. The microwave oven that cost 176 hours of labor by the average factory worker in 1967 cost only 15 hours in 1998. The amount of work time required to purchase the gasoline to drive a car 100 miles dropped from 49 minutes in 1970 to 25 minutes in 1999. The 25-inch color television set that cost the equivalent of a factory worker's wages for a month in 1962 cost only three days' pay in 1998. This rising level of affluence fed the demand for more freedom and greater control over one's destiny. The civil rights movement, the call for removal of the glass ceiling over women in the labor force, the revolts on the university campuses, the increasing power of the teachers' unions, and the emergence of the nondenominational megachurch represented the same basic theme. The people were demanding more control over their own lives. The Port Huron Statement voiced the hopes of many more people than a few dozen university students.

The decades following the publication of the Port Huron Statement also brought the relocation of most of those mature adults of the 1960s who had dismissed that protest as nothing more than the rantings of a radical fringe group. Some relocated to retirement centers and others to nursing homes, but most relocated to cemeteries.

By the end of the 1990s, many of the college and university students of 1962 had become grandparents. As they approached retirement, they were among the leading advocates of pension reform, of making the delivery of health-care services more consumer-oriented, of stricter legislation to reduce consumer fraud, and of expanding the choices available to the public.

The six years prior to the issuance of the Port Huron Statement coincided with the peak of the biggest baby boom in American history. These six years of 1956–61 inclusive brought 25.2 million live births. During the next four decades these babies were reared and socialized in a culture that taught that participation in local, state, and national decision-making processes was not a privilege, but the birthright of every American citizen. President Lyndon B. Johnson's model cities program demanded the "maximum feasible participation" of all residents who would be affected by these federally financed programs. A few years later, in 1975–76 Jimmy Carter proved that a politician could win the nomination for the presidency of a major political party without the support of most of the leaders of that party.

Those babies born in the 1950s and 1960s grew up in a culture that was moving the rights of consumers ahead of the privileges of producers. Just as they voted with their feet in choosing a church home, so also they have become the decisive group in the current national ecclesiastical referendum that is defining (a) the future role of denominational systems and (b) the outcome of the current competition between very large congregations and the other churches for the participation of younger generations of churchgoers.

The year 1962 brought another landmark statement that supported consumerism. This one came from the United States Supreme Court. On March 26, 1962, it ruled that the Court did have jurisdiction over the apportionment of seats in state legislatures. This decision in *Baker v. Carr* opened the door for the decision in *Reynolds v. Sims* in which the Court ruled in 1964 that both houses in a state legislature must be apportioned on the basis of population.[7]

Several of the mainline Protestant denominations are organized to overrepresent small churches and underrepresent the very large congregations in the annual meetings of the regional judicatories. Some of us expected that these two Supreme Court decisions would motivate these denominations to a new formula based on one member, one vote. We were wrong! In several regional judicatories the decision was to adopt a formula that guaranteed an even greater degree of overrepresentation for the small churches. One consequence has been to increase the degree of alienation among the younger members—and staff—of the very large congregations from their denominational system. Another consequence has been to enhance the comparative attractiveness of the very large nondenominational church. Decisions do have consequences!

In 1998, McDonald's decided to invest an estimated $200 million in remodeling the kitchens in its fast-food restaurants. For nearly a half century the company had followed "the producer knows best" appproach. The combination of an occasional new product plus a huge advertising budget plus the opening of new restaurants had been the keys to the continued expansion of its market. In the mid-1990s, however, Burger King became a more threatening competitor when it introduced the idea that every sandwich should be prepared to match the customer's wishes. Subsequently McDonald's concluded that the time had come to be more responsive to the consumer. Their new "Made for You" system promises every sandwich will be prepared one at a time, and customized to the demands of the consumer.

The parallel in the churches is from the producer-created "one size fits all" program package to customized counseling services for each congregation that wants customized advice.

Another consequence of consumerism is a rise in the level of competition among the producers of goods and services. General Motors, Ford Motor Company, and Chrysler began to experience this in the 1950s and 1960s with the competition from German and Japanese automobiles. CBS, ABC, and NBC began to experience this in television with the coming of cable and new networks.

The erosion of inherited denominational loyalties; the disappearance of neighborhood institutions such as pharmacies, banks, motion picture theaters, elementary schools, hardware stores and churches; the decrease in the power of kinship ties;

the increase in interfaith and interdenominational marriages; the emergence of the large regional church as the successor to the neighborhood congregation; and the rise in the use of the private motor vehicle have combined with the growth of consumerism to raise the level of competition among the churches in reaching newcomers to the community and younger generations.

THE RISE OF OUTSOURCING

For generations Americans have been taught that agencies providing religious, educational, and social services should, by definition, be nonprofit organizations. One consequence was that critics argued that a more "businesslike" approach would encourage greater efficiency and economy. The typical response was, "That would be inappropriate. In the business world the bottom line can be measured in the profit-and-loss statement, but that is not our bottom line. We exist to meet people's needs, not to make money."

During the turbulent 1960s the federal government entered into partnership with a variety of nonprofit organizations to expand the range of social services available to people, especially in the large central cities. But these were still partnerships of nonprofit agencies with nonprofit organizations.

The 1990s, however, brought the words *outsourcing* and *privatization* into widespread usage. Local governments now hire for-profit companies to pick up garbage, plow snow, search for candidates to fill a vacant position, repair streets, and install new equipment. Instead of doing the work with their own staff, they outsource that particular task. Welfare reform encouraged states to outsource most of the work required to move welfare clients into the workforce. The United States government now outsources much of its disaster-relief efforts on other continents.

One of the most significant facets of privatization can be

illustrated by two sets of statistics. During the late 1990s the number of Americans using government-issued food stamps dropped by more than one-third. Concurrently the number of privately operated food pantries and soup kitchens skyrocketed and now provides over $1 billion worth of food annually to 20 million needy persons. In New York City, for example, the number of soup kitchens and food pantries rose from fewer than 40 in 1980 to 600 in 1992 and 6,100 in 1999. Nationally that number has grown to over 40,000 in 1999.[8]

In the religious music sector, much of the contemporary Christian music is originating with private companies or partnerships. It is not originating in congregational or denominational circles. Congregations ask for bids to operate the bookstore or the weekday child-care facility or to provide the Sunday noon meal or to provide janitorial services. Frequently that contract is awarded to a for-profit bidder.

Denominations are outsourcing many of their continuing education programs, and at least a couple are outsourcing contracts for planting new missions or for training mission-developer pastors or for running the annual denominational national youth rally.

This entry of for-profit organizations into what once was exclusively a nonprofit world is a consequence of marketplace competition combined with the need for greater success in meeting the demands of consumers.[9] Will congregations begin to outsource their search for a new senior pastor? For help in planning and administering a capital funds campaign? For responding to the call for a new hymnal? For a weekend retreat center experience for a cadre of leaders? For counsel in planning the next chapter in their ministry? For specialized training for volunteer leaders? For reinventing their organizational structure? For transforming their teaching ministries? For creating new worship experiences for new generations? For advice on designing an interactive web site? Or will they rely on denominational resources?

If next year turns out to be 1952, the probable answer is that they will rely on denominational assistance. If, however, next year turns out to be 2001 or 2003 or 2009, they are more likely to rely on outsourcing.

WHAT IS ACCEPTABLE?

Perhaps the most subtle consequence of consumerism is the raising of the bar to qualify as acceptable. Many of today's church shoppers refer to relevance, quality, and choices as they identify the criteria they used in choosing a church home. Geographical convenience, denominational affiliation, and kinfolk ties rarely rank higher than fourth or fifth. The congregation that earned a grade of 70 on relevance, quality, and choices in 1960 today must earn a grade of 80 to 85 to be competitive in that never-ending effort to reach new generations of potential churchgoers.

Consumerism is more than an unwelcome trend. Consumerism has radically transformed the relationship between producers of goods and services and the people who constitute the market for those goods and services.

QUALITY IS NOT CHEAP!

How much money is required to pay all of the financial obligations of the typical Protestant congregation? If those obligations do not include substantial capital expenditures for debt service or construction, and if they do not include a large amount (more than 25 percent of all expenditures) for benevolences, a useful beginning point at the end of the 1990s was $1,000 times the average worship attendance for the year. This estimate should be adjusted up or down, depending on distinctive local circumstances. For most congregations with a full-time resident pastor and no substantial capital expenditures, this comes to $17 to $25 per worshiper per week. Thus

90

the family of three needs to drop $50 to $75 in the offering plate every week they are present if the church's bills are to be paid out of contributions.

How much is $20 per week per worshiper? That is approximately twelve times the $1.50 to $2.00 per worshiper required to pay the weekly bills back in 1965. The Consumer Price Index in 1999 was approximately 5.5 times the 1965 level. Per capita personal income in the United States in current dollars in 1999 was approximately eight times the average in 1965.

One of the consequences of consumerism is that the cost of church has risen faster than the increase in people's incomes.

One of the consequences of consumerism is that the cost of church has risen faster than the increase in people's incomes. Today's churchgoers, especially those born after 1950, are looking for relevance, quality, and choices. Relevance, quality, and choices cost money! One way to cover those increased costs is to spread them over a larger participation base. The old dream was that per-unit costs would go down as size went up. That was called "economy of scale." The new reality is that costs per one hundred people at worship usually go up as size goes up. But one reason for that increase in size is a recognition of the importance of relevance, quality, and choices. The increased size is one way to cover those higher costs.

WHO CONTROLS THE DESTINATION OF THE CHARITABLE DOLLAR?

This introduces what many critics of contemporary consumerism identify as the most regrettable consequence. If the cost of church has increased twelve times in one-third of a century while the average per-capita personal income has risen only eightfold, how can a congregation or a denomination cover that gap? One response is to reduce expenditures. A second is to focus on teaching stewardship. A third is to ignore the call for relevance, quality, and choices.

A fourth alternative accentuates the gap between the producers of goods and services and the consumers of those goods and services. This is called "designated second-mile giving." In the pre-consumerism era, the consumers were expected to send their taxes, benevolence giving, fees, dues, and other financial resources to the producers of the services. The officials of that agency (municipality, school district, university, voluntary association, denominational agency, congregation, etc.) would decide in specific detail on the allocation of those dollars.

In recent decades, a growing proportion of the consumers who contributed those dollars decided they deserved an active voice in the allocation of those scarce resources. In municipal government this transfer of power from producers to consumers may be in the form of a referendum on a bond issue or a new taxing district or an assessment or voter approval for an increase in the tax rate.

In the churches the response to the demand for a more influential consumer voice in the destination of the charitable dollar is the increase in designated giving. It is not unusual today for a congregation to encourage its constituents to contribute to (1) the operating budget, (2) the building fund, and (3) one or more of thirty to sixty special causes and needs.[10] From a pragmatic perspective, this is a quick and simple way to increase total member contributions by 30 to 70 percent.

A common rule of thumb is that a characteristic of a healthy small to midsize Protestant congregation is that 33 percent of the member households will account for 67 percent of the contributions from members. The larger the size of the congregation, however, and the greater the reliance on designated giving, the more likely there will be a greater spread between those two numbers. In the very large congregation that challenges people with thirty to seventy specific needs for designated second-mile giving, it is not unusual for 15 to 20 percent of the constituent households to account for 70 to 90 percent of the total dollar receipts in a given year. Is that good or bad? Is that largely a product of the fact that in many mega-churches the people are widely scattered all along the spectrum that reflects commitment? Is that gap a reflection of a broad spread in the income levels of the constituents? Or is it generational? Or is the number-one factor a consequence of consumerism?

Another consequence, from a congregational perspective, is the increasing proportion of money that comes from nonmembers. Membership and financial support are becoming unrelated variables.

Another consequence, from a congregational perspective, is the increasing proportion of money that comes from non-members. Membership and financial support are becoming unrelated variables. One facet of this is the congregation with a very high threshold for people seeking to become members. With 200 confirmed members, the average attendance at worship fluctuates between 600 and 700. Slightly over one-half of the annual dollar contributions come from these 200 members, and the balance comes from the 1,200 "constituents" who worship there with varying degrees of frequency.

A more common example is the congregation that receives approximately one-half of its annual financial receipts from resident members, a tenth from members who have retired to the Sunbelt but still retain their church membership "back home," another one-fifth from resident constituents who have chosen not to become members, and the other one-fifth from "friends" who listen to that congregation's radio program or view the televised worship services.

A third example is the capital funds campaign in which three of the five largest contributions come from (1) a widow in another state who is delighted her son and family are active and enthusiastic members of this church, (2) a wealthy member of another congregation in town who is a close golfing friend of the pastor, and (3) a couple in another state who worship here twice a year while visiting friends and who have become favorably impressed with the life and ministry of this congregation.

Consumerism has made the old rule books on church finances obsolete.

From a denominational perspective, one consequence of consumerism is the erosion of denominational loyalties. A second is a greater dependence on appeals for designated contributions for specific denominational causes such as missions, the funding of pension programs, and capital expenditures. A third can be seen in those religious traditions that have responded to the decrease in receipts from congregations by identifying and enlisting individual donors who can and will make a substantial gift to a specific cause.

This is transforming the role and responsibilities of the chief executive of the regional denominational judicatory and requires a revision of the old rule book. Several years ago the care of pastors and the resolution of internal conflict in congregational life were added to that list. The newest addition is the capability and willingness to identify and cultivate individuals, family foundations, and other potential donors who can make a substantial financial contribution to the annual budget of that regional judicatory and/or to a special project such as new church development. In commenting on this, the senior pastor of a large United Methodist congregation said, "We expect our new bishop should be raising at least $3 million annually in special gifts from individuals by the end of his third year here."

THE THREAT TO INSTITUTIONS

Perhaps the most subtle consequence of consumerism is the threat to institutions. The self-identified "political independent" undermines the role of the organized political parties. The relatively high rate of divorce undermines that institution called the family. The rapid numerical growth of the independent churches undermines the role of denominational systems. Parental discontent undermines the public schools. Consumerism has transformed the criteria for the public evaluation of institutions of higher education. Consumerism has undermined the economic viability of the traditional Main Street lined with retail stores. Free agency has threatened the future of major league baseball and basketball teams. The widespread ownership of the private motor vehicle has undermined the traditional geographical definition of neighborhood. Televison has made it more difficult for voluntary associations to compete for people's discretionary time. Consumerism has undermined the labor movement.

If one accepts the generalization that for social institutions in American culture to thrive, all legitimate institutions also must thrive, consumerism can be described as a threat to both congregational life and denominational systems as well as to other voluntary associations.

CAMPUS MINISTRIES

One of the most widely ignored consequences of consumerism is in the design of denominationally funded ministries with undergraduates in the nation's colleges and universities. In 1999 only one out of five of all the students in these institutions of higher education were both (a) under twenty-two years of age and (b) full-time students.

The young and full-time students who were the primary constituents of the campus ministries of the 1950s and early 1960s have largely disappeared. Many also brought with them a powerful loyalty to the religious tradition to which they had been reared. They have been replaced by huge numbers of consumers of all ages, many with a part-time or full-time job.

The students of the 1950s came expecting to participate in a program designed and produced by the professionals. The consumers of the late 1990s come with a variety of competing demands on their time, energy, and loyalty, but without that guiding denominational loyalty.

One consequence of this shift is that efforts to perpetuate or to re-create that producer-designed ministry with under-graduates born in the pre-1945 era is seldom effective in reaching today's consumers on campus who were born after 1975. The effective contemporary campus ministries are playing that game by a new rule book, rather than by attempting to recruit players who will be comfortable with the old one. Most of the contributors to the new rule books for campus ministries came from the parachurch organizations or from the leaders of very large churches with a high priority on ministries with people from a nearby college or university.

AMBIGUITY OR CERTAINTY?

One of the most subtle, but also one of the profound, consequences of consumerism is a product of the increase in the number and variety of choices offered the consumer. That four-stage sequence can be summarized very simply. Consumerism leads to an expansion of choices. Choice leads to an affirmation of pluralism. Pluralism leads to greater uncertainty about what is the "correct" or "right" alternative. The greater the degree of ambivalence about what is good, right, proper, correct, appropriate, and orthodox, the greater the demand for certainty. The greater the degree of ambivalence, the more likely highly divisive quarrels will result from varying interpretations of the rule book.

That sequence can be illustrated by political strategies, the current debate over vouchers for elementary school children, organized religion, the birth of new Christian movements, advertising, the delivery of health-care services, the demand by patients for second opinions, the growing market for consumer publications that will inform the customer what are the "best buys," and alternative strategies for responding to the threat of international terrorism.

The lure of pluralism versus the quest for certainty also can be seen in the small to middle-sized congregation that boasts, "Our strength is in our diversity," and watches passively as the vast majority of first-time Sunday morning visitors do not return, but eventually join a church that emphasizes certainty, internal consistency, and clarity in its proclamation of the gospel.

This conflict between an affirmation of pluralism and a total absense of ambiguity in the belief system is at the heart of the internal conflict that has been so disruptive in several American denominational systems in recent decades. The only quarrel over that basic generalization is whether the Roman Catholic Church, the Southern Baptist Convention, the Lutheran Church-Missouri Synod, the Episcopal Church, The United Methodist Church, the Presbyterian Church (U.S.A.), the Evangelical Lutheran Church in America, or the Christian Reformed Church should be at the top of the list of examples.

From this observer's perspective, four recent related trends merit mention. First is the sharp increase in the number of churchgoers who prefer certainty over ambiguity in a congregation's belief system. This is especially pronounced among the generations born after 1945. Second, several mainline

Protestant denominations have sought to affirm their self-image as pluralistic religious bodies.[11] Third, in order to minimize offending, and perhaps losing, members they feel they cannot afford to lose, most small congregations established before 1960 tend to avoid choosing up sides over this question of ambiguity versus certainty—and thus are often perceived to be on the side of ambiguity.

Fourth, most, but not all, very large congregations follow one of two strategies in responding to this growing demand for certainty.

One strategy is to proclaim with great clarity and absolute precision, "This is what we believe and what we teach." They play by a set of clearly written and precisely stated rules. This is easiest for the independent or nondenominational congregation, since it does not have to compete with a national stereotype of what that denomination believes and teaches or what is included in that denomination's rule book.

A second, and more complex, strategy begins with an affirmation of the differences among people and the capability to conceptualize this as a congregation of congregations.

Which is the more pleasing to God in worship? Classical Christian music? Contemporary Christian music?

Should the primary focus in worship be on praising and worshiping God? Or on how the gospel speaks to the concerns that people bring to church? Or on persuading the nonbeliever, the pilgrim, the skeptic, the self-identified agnostic, the seeker, and the searcher of the truth and relevance of the Christian faith?

Should the sermon challenge deeply committed believers to advance one more step in their faith pilgrimage and become transformed into fully devoted disciples of Jesus Christ? Or should the focus be on helping new Christians become more knowledgeable about their faith?

What is the right answer to each of these three contemporary questions?

A growing number of congregations are avoiding the "either/or" fork in the road and are offering one or more worship experiences every weekend organized around contemporary Christian music while also offering one or more traditional services. One or more may devote most of the time to prayer, praising God, and proclaiming the word while another devotes 30 to 45 minutes to a sermon designed to help the worshipers understand how Scripture speaks to their personal and spiritual concerns. Or the weekend schedule may include five different worship experiences: one for seekers, one for new believers, one for learners, one for those ready to be transformed into disciples, and one for disciples ready to be challenged to become apostles.

What is right, correct, and appropriate for one group may not be timely, relevant, or appropriate for another group. One response is to create a three- or four-paragraph rule book that delegates huge quantities of trust to the contemporary leadership.

The obvious implication is that the very large congregation is better prepared to act like a congregation of congregations than are small and middle-sized churches.

Thus the quest for certainty has contributed to a more supportive societal context for the emergence of more megachurches. In broader terms, one consequence of competition is that it has placed many small institutions on the list of endangered species. That list includes the small dairy farm, the corner drugstore, the physician in solo practice, the five-and-dime variety store on Main Street, the 160-acre wheat farm, the motel owned and operated by a married couple, and the small church.

Whether the growth of consumerism has turned out to be a net plus or a net minus for American society will be influenced by the value system of the person making that evaluation. No one can deny, however, that consumerism has radically transformed the context for parish ministry.

Whether those changes strengthen the role of the very large congregation or undermine it will be determined largely by how the leaders respond.

The big issue, however, is not whether one applauds or disapproves of the growth of consumerism. The central issue is that consumerism is now a fact of life, and this raises the question of how your congregation will respond to this change in the societal context. The consequences of consumerism are real, and they have radically transformed the context for the parish ministry. Do you identify this new context as a source of despair? Or as a challenge to your creativity? Perhaps the most significant single example of this is how the churches will respond to the contemporary quest for community.

THE LOSS OF COMMUNITY

Several variables have combined in recent decades to erode the traditional geographically defined sense of community. Ray Oldenburg offers a simple but exceptionally provocative insight into an understanding of community.[12] In the best of communities, participants rely on first-person pronouns such as "we," "us," and "ours." Consumerism has encouraged the use of first- and third-person pronouns such as "mine" and "theirs." Instead of drawing vertical lines that emphasize sharing, consumerism articulates lines of demarcation that separate "us" from "them." Over one-half of today's Americans were born since we began to erode the foundations of the traditional definition of community.

In 1939 the United States was served by 235,000 public schools. In most of them the parents were acquainted with the teachers, and most children could call every other pupil correctly by name by the end of September. By 1998 that number had been reduced to 85,000 public schools. In only a few could a parent know every teacher. Anonymity and complexity had replaced intimacy and simplicity. A growing proportion of parents identified the public school as an adversary rather than as an ally. The public school no longer is a foundation for building a sense of community.

As recently as the 1960s, people went outdoors after a hot summer day to enjoy the cool of the evening. That made it easy to socialize with the neighbors. Today the heat drives people indoors to enjoy their air conditioning. The front porch has been replaced by the deck in the backyard. Homebuilders once sold shelter. Today they sell privacy and space for private entertainment. The "starter house" for first-time home buyers in 1999 contained nearly three times as many square feet of space as its counterpart five decades earlier. Instead of walking with a few friends to the nearby neighborhood motion picture theater, it is easier to stay home and watch a videotape.

The increase in the number of mothers employed outside the home, the increase in the number of adults working for two employers, and the lengthening of the journey to work have moved the place where one meets and makes new friends from the neighborhood to the place of work, to the school campus, to places of recreation, and to a variety of voluntary associations. As recently as the 1960s millions of Americans had neighbors who worked in the same building. People saw their friends at work and in the neighborhood. These repeated contacts, brief as most of them were, reinforced the fabric of one's personal friendship circle. It also was relatively easy to organize a four- or five-person car pool—and the daily car pool provided another opportunity for bonding. The decentralization of housing and of jobs makes it difficult to organize a car pool of even three persons today. The highly redundant system of strengthening one's social network has been undermined by the fragmentation of contemporary lifestyles.

WHERE IS THE THIRD PLACE?

In a remarkably wise and provocative book, a Florida sociologist, Ray Oldenburg, has provided a conceptual framework for looking at community.[13] Oldenburg has suggested that most adults in North America and Europe organize their lives around three places. The first place is the home. A good home provides a healthy, supportive, and predictable environment for rearing children. The identity of the adults in the home often can be described by such words as *wife, husband, mother, father, disciplinarian, breadwinner, parent, spouse, stepson, in-law, grandmother,* or *half sister.*

The second place in the lives of many adults is the place of work. Here one's identity often is described by job title, expertise, professional competence, the workday, compensation, or duties.

The third place is the focal point of Oldenburg's book. He describes the third place as "the core settings of informal public life . . . that host the regular, voluntary, informal, and happily anticipated gatherings of individuals beyond the realm of home and work." The neighborhood tavern is one of Oldenburg's favorite examples of a good third place, but the number of neighborhood taverns has shrunk by at least 60 percent since 1960. That is a reflection of the fact that today's third place rarely can be identified in geographical terms. Fewer and fewer adults "neighbor" with people who reside nearby.

A good third place is where a person is identified by who one is as a person, not by what one does for a living or by kinship ties. For some farmers in the early years of this century, it was a couple of hours in the blacksmith shop or in the hardware store on Saturday morning. For thousands of today's teenage boys, the gang is their third place. For many choir members, the number-one third place in their life is the weeknight choir rehearsal. For others, it may be a bowling league or a service club or a softball team or a bridge club or a book group or a coffee shop or a minor league baseball park.

The crucial distinctive characteristic of a good third place in today's world is that participants eagerly look forward to being with that same group of people in that familiar setting. It is increasingly difficult to identify the participants by the geographical proximity of their places of residence. That group of baseball fans who sit together in the same section of the bleachers may come from a twenty-mile radius.

For the workaholic, the place of work may be today's third place. For hundreds of "snowbirds," the winter residence on the west coast of Florida or in the valley in Arizona or Texas is their third place.

For millions of long-tenured church members, that congregation is their third place. They eagerly anticipate Sunday morning as a reunion with dear friends they have not seen for several days. This pattern is most clearly visible among some of the older adults in smaller congregations who now live alone and are not employed outside the home.

For millions of long-tenured church members, that congregation is their third place. They eagerly anticipate Sunday morning as a reunion with dear friends they have not seen for several days.

For others, the third place is that adult Sunday school class they helped to organize back in the mid-1960s. For many older women, the circle in the women's organization is a favorite third place. For a few, it is working in the church kitchen. For a growing number, it is that small Bible study-prayer group they helped to start several years ago. In a growing number of congregations, the current third places include the mutual support groups created by the leaders of that parish. For some teenagers with few friends in school, their third place is the youth fellowship. For several young never-married adults, their favorite third place is working with friends on construction of a Habitat For Humanity House. For many it is Wednesday night at church where the schedule begins with a meal and includes a dozen or more groups, classes, meetings, and other gatherings. For a couple of dozen fathers, the new third place is that Saturday morning Bible study and prayer group they launched after attending a Promise Keepers weekend. The singles group that meets every Friday evening is the third place for many, most of whom are formerly married. For at least a few pastors, their third place is that Tuesday morning with a half dozen other ministers organized around fellowship, coffee, candor, structured Bible study, sermon preparation, mutual support, and unneeded calories.

For some church members, church is strictly a religious place. For others, it is primarily the great good third place in their lives. For many adults, church is a combination of spiritual nurture and a great good place.

FIVE OBVIOUS IMPLICATIONS

What does this concept mean to your congregation? Five implications stand out. First, what are the criteria the first-time visitor uses to decide whether to return next week? For some, the answer is simple: Will this church provide a relevant response to my spiritual needs? For at least a few, however, the number-one criterion is whether this church appears to be a promising third place for me. Other first-time visitors use both criteria in deciding whether to return next week.

A second implication becomes most highly visible when the new pastor turns out to be a serious mismatch. The gifts, skills, priorities, personality, and place on the theological spectrum of the new minister simply do not match what the members seek. Some leave for another church home, others simply drop out, but many stay. Who leaves? Those who first of all perceive the church in religious terms. Who stays? Those for whom this congregation is a great good third place.

Third, which congregations are most effective in assimilating a flood of new members? Those parishes that are able to (a) immediately help newcomers find an established good third place within that congregation and/or (b) enlist newcomers in helping to pioneer the creation of a new third place. In more precise terms, these are the churches that conceptualize themselves as either a congregation of congregations or as a congregation of communities.

Fourth, as families leave for home after church, who are the first persons to reach their car, and who are the ones they wait for impatiently to join them? Those who perceive church to be an important third place are reluctant to leave. Those who see the church as primarily or only as a religious place are the first to reach their car.

Finally, does the rule book followed by your congregation recognize and affirm the importance of a third place in the lives of people? Two common examples of a conflict between the affirmation of that third place and a congregational rule book are (a) asking continuing groups to change their weekly meeting place from this room to that room every year or two and (b) forced rotation ("fruit basket turnover") of members of a circle in the women's organization or in adult classes.

At this point, it would be tempting to conclude this chapter with two questions. First, do you want people to perceive your congregation as an attractive third place in their lives? Second, if yes, what are you doing to strengthen the attractiveness of those third places?

That, however, would overlook a significant recent trend.

Back in 1950, one out of every ten households included only one person. Today that proportion is one out of four. In actual numbers, the change has been from fewer than 5 million residents of one-person households in 1950 to nearly 11 million in 1970 to 25 million in 1995. Add to those 25 million the more than 11 million one-parent families and compare that number with the 25 million two-parent families with one or more children under age eighteen at home.

What do those numbers add up to in terms of this discussion? Millions of churchgoers who look to the church to be the first, not the third, place in their life! For them, home is a place to sleep, but it does not meet their needs for a predictable, supportive, and healthy first place. A place to sleep is not the equivalent of a supportive first place. When asked to describe their church, they define it as "my family" or "my only support system" or as "where I feel loved, understood, and cared for."

While the leaders rarely discuss it in these terms, a growing number of congregations have become the first place in the lives of many people. Ray Oldenburg defines a good third place as "a home away from home." That definition presumes the existence of a home. For many who do not enjoy the security, the comfort, the support, and the fellowship of "home," the church has become their home away from where they sleep. This definition of their church comes from the thirty-five-year-old, never-married adult; the sixteen-year-old living with a stepparent; the single man who moved here because of a job transfer; the seventy-year-old widow; the single-parent mother; the man and woman who met here in this church and are now engaged to be married; the empty-nest couple who reared their children in this church; and the spouse who is half of a long-distance marriage separated by a couple of hundred or more miles. For them, church is the first place, not the third place, in their life.

If the combination of the disappearance of the traditional geographically defined neighborhood and the power of consumerism are undermining the sense of community, what is the most promising place to look for a new expression of community? The small "We are one big family" congregation? The singles bar? The workplace? The golf course? Or the megachurch that conceptualizes itself as a congregation of communities? (See chapter 7.)

CHAPTER FOUR

Why So Few?

During the second half of the twentieth century, the number of very large Protestant congregations averaging 800 or more at weekend worship more than tripled to an estimated 5,000-6,000 by the end of 1999.

From this observer's perspective, the demand by churchgoers is sufficient to support at least twice that many very large congregations. This raises a fundamental question: If both the need and the demand justify the existence of at least 12,000 very large congregations, why are there so few? Like many simple questions, this one requires a multifaceted explanation.

THE POWER OF PATH DEPENDENCY

Back in 1985, Professor Paul David, a Stanford University economist, introduced into economic theory a concept called "path dependency." This theory states that once people, or institutions, begin to travel down a certain path, it is very difficult for them to choose a new road. Professor David used the adherence to the QWERTY arrangement of typewriter keyboards as an example. In the 1930s, August Dvorak designed a new keyboard arrangement that placed the most frequently used pairs of letters on one row. This arrangement made it easier for people to learn how to type and enabled typists to increase their speed. Path dependency, however, has perpetuated the QWERTY arrangement.

A similar explanation can be offered to explain why farmers continued to plant wheat during the dry years of the 1920s and 1930s in Oklahoma, even though a crop failure became an annual event.

Path dependency also can be used to explain why military leaders often have prepared their armies to fight an earlier war, why people left homeless by a flood choose to rebuild on that same floodplain, why Microsoft's MS-DOS operating system became the standard for personal computers rather than Apple's Macintosh, why Value Jet flight 592 carried hazardous cargo, and why the congregation averaging 145 at worship in 1965 was averaging 135 three decades later after the population of that community had increased sixfold.

While a new generation of economists have published criticisms of path dependency theory, it continues to help explain why there are so few very large congregations in American Protestantism.

THE ECCLESIASTICAL CULTURE

Overlapping path dependency, and probably more influential and even more widely ignored, is the ecclesiastical culture of a particular religious tradition. In a few denominations that ecclesiastical culture is supportive of very large congregations. Examples include the Evangelical Presbyterian Church, the Christian Church and Churches of Christ, the Roman Catholic Church, the Reformed Church in America, and the Evangelical Free Church. The number-one example, however, of an ecclesiastical culture that is supportive of the very large congregation can be found in hundreds of very large independent or nondenominational churches.

By contrast, the ecclesiastical culture of several religious traditions in America provides a supportive institutional environment for small to middle-sized congregations, but a hostile institutional context for the emergence and/or continued numerical growth of very large congregations. Examples include the Church of the Brethren, the Free Methodist Church, The United Methodist Church, the Episcopal Church, the Wesleyan Church, the Wisconsin Evangelical

Lutheran Synod, several Mennonite and Quaker traditions, the Evangelical Lutheran Church in America, the United Church of Christ, the Christian Church (Disciples of Christ), the Associate Reformed Presbyterian Church, the Cumberland Presbyterian Church, and the Universal Fellowship of Metropolitan Community Churches.

This point can be illustrated by a brief look at what is now The United Methodist Church. In 1965 the former Methodist Church included 47 congregations that reported an average worship attendance of 1,200 or more. Thirty years later only 13 of those 47 congregations reported an average worship attendance of 1,200 or more. Of the 60 largest Methodist congregations in 1965, a total of 33 had experienced a decrease of at least 50 percent in worship attendance by 1995. In many of these congregations the sharpest drop in worship attendance followed the arrival of a new pastor.

This hostile ecclesiastical environment for large United Methodist congregations is most highly visible in the Northeast, the Midwest, and the West. In California, for example, in 1965 a total of 62 Methodist congregations reported an average worship attendance of 500 or more. By 1996 that number had dropped to 14. That decrease coincided with (a) an increase from 18.6 million to 31.67 million in the population of California and (b) the emergence of scores of Protestant megachurches in that state.

In Ohio the parallel numbers were 66 large Methodist congregations in 1965 and 24 in 1996, in Illinois 39 and 17, in Wisconsin 14 and 3, in the Northeastern Jurisdiction 94 and 43, and in the Western Jurisdiction 91 and 41.

Among the most influential qualities of that hostile ecclesiastical environment are short pastorates, planting new missions designed to be small churches, distrust of local leadership, the absence of a clearly defined religious identity, a low threshold for those seeking to become church members, an assumption that theological schools will prepare students for both ordination and effective service as parish pastors, a heavy reliance on financial subsidies, a geographical definition of the parish to be served by a particular church, a policy of "promoting" pastors of smaller congregations to become senior ministers of larger churches, the expectation that a primary role of the very large congregation is to send money to denominational headquarters, an overrepresentation of people from small churches in denominational policy-making meetings, and a fear that the existence of large congregations will threaten the future of small churches.

It is difficult to grow large churches in an ecclesiastical culture that follows a rule book that penalizes growth and rewards shrinkage!

HOW MANY FISH IN THE POND?

"The potential for our congregation to become a megachurch is zero," declared a longtime leader at Bethany Church. "The north-south length of this county is about twenty miles, and east-west is about forty miles. The county seat is near the center, and we have a population of slightly over 40,000. Another 20,000 people are scattered across the rest of the county, including a couple of small cities and several villages. That's 60,000 people spread over 800 square miles. The last count I heard was there are about 120 churches in this county. That's 1 for every 500 residents. When you add the fact that about half of these 60,000 residents don't have any active church affiliation, that means an average potential of 250 residents per church, and that includes children. There are only so many fish in this pond, and a lot of churches are fishing for more members. At Bethany we now average approximately 700 at worship, and that makes us one of the four or five largest Protestant churches in the county. It also means that on the typical Sunday morning, slightly over 1 percent of all residents worship with us. One pastor told me recently that

the combined average church attendance of all 120 congregations in this county is approximately 18,000. That means we at
Bethany have nearly 4 percent of the churchgoers on the average weekend. For us to become a megachurch averaging 1,400
at worship would require us to attract 8 percent of the churchgoers on the typical weekend. There simply are too few fish in
this pond for us to grow into a megachurch!"

These comments raise three issues that merit discussion.
The first, and the most obvious, is the power of expectations.
Low expectations usually produce limited results. High expectations are more likely to produce high performance. Neutral
expectations really do not exist.

The second issue is, How large is the circle. How large is
the area that you expect your congregation to serve? In 1920
the typical answer was, "People living within a mile or two of
our church." By 1955 the radius of that circle had been
extended to three to five miles. By 1999 literally thousands of
American Protestant churches were serving a constituency
scattered across a circle with a radius of ten to fifteen miles
from the meeting place. A few megachurches described their
service area as a circle with a thirty-mile radius.

The basic generalization, and this applies to center-city
churches, to suburban congregations, and to small-town and
rural parishes, is that the larger the average worship attendance becomes, the larger the circle needs to be.

The third issue is the density of the population. A circle
with a ten-mile radius may include only several hundred residents or it may include more than a million people. The basic
generalization is that the larger the number of residents per
square mile, the smaller the percentage any one congregation
will be able to reach and serve.

How does this translate into operational terms? The following six examples illustrate the impact of both the size of
that circle and the density of the population. These are not
offered as norms, but as not-uncommon patterns.

1. 25 percent of the adults living within a mile of the meeting place regularly worship with that congregation.
2. 15 percent of the adults living within a three-mile radius regularly worship with that congregation.
3. 10 percent of the adults living within a five-mile radius regularly worship with that congregation.
4. 3 percent of the adults living within a ten-mile radius regularly worship with that congregation.
5. 1 percent of the adults living within a twenty-five-mile radius regularly worship with that congregation.
6. 0.3 percent of the adults living within a thirty-five-mile radius regularly worship with that congregation.

If Bethany Church expects to double its average worship attendance, each weekend it will have to attract approximately 4 percent of the 35,000 residents, ages fourteen and over, living within twenty miles of that meeting place. That is a **big** challenge. It can be done, however, and several megachurches are doing it; but achievement is a product of the combination of high expectations, very high-quality ministries, a surplus of off-street parking, a creative staff, and an extensive seven-day-a-week program.

An alternative would be to fish in two places in that pond. This strategy calls for one congregation with one staff, one budget, one treasury, one name, and several weekend worship experiences at two sites. Worship attendance might average 1,000 at one site and 800 to 1,200 at the other location.[1]

The real barrier is not the number of fish in the pond. The real barrier is the self-imposed ceiling created by low expectations.

SCARCITY OR ABUNDANCE?

A joke among Presbyterians can be condensed into two parts.

Question: What is the primary responsibility of the Session in a Presbyterian church?

Answer: To tell other people what they cannot do.

That introduces a fourth part of this explanation for the relatively small number of very large churches in American Protestantism. A crucial barrier to becoming a very large congregation often is in the system of governance.

Two assumptions shape the system of governance in at least 90 percent of the congregations in American Protestantism. The one that is rarely discussed is the guiding assumption that a congregation's role is limited by the scarcity of resources. These resources include the number of lay volunteers, money, meeting rooms, off-street parking, the pastor's time and energy, the number of hours in the week, enthusiasm, an openness to new ideas, creativity, passion, commitment, potential future new members, hours of sunshine, and the distance people will travel to church.

The second assumption, while less common, is equally influential. This is the assumption that every member, faction, group, organization, and class should be represented, either directly or indirectly, in policy making. In the more extreme expression of this system of governance, every proposal for change must be approved at a congregational meeting. Since it usually is easier to mobilize people around opposition to change than it is to motivate them to support

> Two assumptions shape the system of governance in at least 90 percent of the congregations in American Protestantism. The one that is rarely discussed is the guiding assumption that a congregation's role is limited by the scarcity of resources.

change, this means the system of governance is biased in favor of the dependency path and against choosing a new road into tomorrow. This helps to explain why it is rare to find a congregation that (1) averages more than 800 at worship and (2) regularly submits every major policy issue to a vote at a congregational meeting.

When taken together these two assumptions bias the system of governance in support of rationing scarce resources and against change.

By contrast, the vast majority of very large congregations operate on the assumption that when God challenges congregations to initiate new ministries to reach more people with the gospel of Jesus Christ, the Lord also will provide the resources required to meet that challenge. Their rule books and their decision-making processes assume an abundance of resources, not a scarcity.

> ✝
> By contrast, the vast majority of very large congregations operate on the assumption that when God challenges congregations to initiate new ministries to reach more people with the gospel of Jesus Christ, the Lord also will provide the resources required to meet that challenge.

Likewise, most very large congregations, in some cases counter to their own constitution or denominational polity, operate on the assumption that (1) leaders are called to lead; (2) not every opinion deserves the same weight as other opinions; (3) informed opinions are more valuable than uninformed opinions; (4) most people naturally will prefer efforts to perpetuate yesterday over challenges to create a new tomorrow; (5) congregations are worshiping communities of people called to follow Christ, not political democracies; (6) the number-one criterion in making decisions in ministry is not, "What do our people here prefer?" but rather, "What would Jesus advocate if he were speaking to us in this room today?"; (7) the larger the number of people actively involved in making a particular decision, the more likely that process will result in a watered-down compromise rather than a bold step into the unknown; and (8) God's call to the vast majority of the members of that very large church is to be engaged in doing ministry, not in attending committee meetings.

One result is the basic generalization that the larger the size of the congregation, the smaller the size of the governing board. Thus the 150-member congregation may have 35 members on the governing board in an attempt to provide direct representation to every group, family tree, faction, age-group, class, and organization. As part of the emphasis on being a pure democracy, as many as 100 to 140 of those 150 members may attend a congregational meeting to vote on an especially divisive issue.

One result is the basic generalization that the larger the size of the congregation, the smaller the size of the governing board.

By contrast, the 1,500-member congregation is more likely to function with a governing board of 7 to 15 adults, including the pastor who has both voice and vote. The central theme is not to be sensitive and responsive to the collective wishes of the members, but rather to challenge and enable every member to be engaged in doing ministry.[2]

THE SHORTAGE OF VISIONARY LEADERS

At least a few readers will contend that the fifth part of this explanation for the small number of very large congregations should be placed first. One reason why it is placed fifth is that the shortage of vision-driven pastors is, at least in part, a product of the power of path dependency. Overlapping that is the simple fact that the combination of path dependency, a hostile ecclesiastical culture, and a restrictive system of congregational governance is a powerful barrier to the emergence of vision-driven leadership.

For this discussion, pastors can be divided into three groups. The first, and the largest group, takes seriously a concept articulated many years ago by James Glasse called "paying the rent."[3] While this may not be the most important obligation, for most pastors it does take precedence over everything else. Glasse defined the rent as (1) preaching and worship, (2) teaching and pastoral care, and (3) organization and administration. He emphasized that paying the rent is not a full-time job!

A pastor should have discretionary time and energy left over after paying the rent. Those discretionary resources can be channeled into family responsibilities, the personal and spiritual growth of the pastor, hobbies, community involvement, the pursuit of an academic degree, challenging the members to help pioneer new ministries, enlisting allies to design and implement strategies to reach the unchurched, working for social justice, denominational responsibilities, serving in elective political office, writing, speaking on the lecture circuit, overpaying the rent, leading workshops, a part-time teaching position in a nearby college or theological school, coaching an athletic team, serving as a volunteer police or hospital chaplain, leading groups on a tour of the Holy Land, surfing the Internet, creating educational materials to be used in that parish, recovery from an addiction, seaching for a new spouse, or some other activity.

116

The decision a pastor makes on the use of those discretionary resources after paying the rent usually will determine whether that will be a maintenance or a mission-driven ministry.

A second, and smaller, group of parish pastors consists of those who fail to pay the rent on time or are not able to pay it in full every month. This may be a result of a lack of professional competence, poor health, the burden of family or marital responsibilities, a product of personality traits or boredom, a consequence of poor work habits, or of uncertainty about a call to the parish ministry. The obvious consequences of not paying the rent in full and/or on time often include a growing cadre of unhappy parishioners and/or the quiet departure of substantial numbers of people and/or relatively few first-time visitors, most of whom do not return, and/or brief pastorates of one to four years and/or a departure of that minister from the parish ministry after one or two pastorates.

When a congregation survives two consecutive pastorates in which the rent has not been paid in full, the local agenda often shifts from a desire to maintain the status quo to a focus on institutional survival. If the next pastor pays the rent in full and on time, the result often is a combination of euphoria and widespread contentment with a maintenance-level ministry.

A third and still smaller group of pastors includes those who (a) pay the rent in full and on time and (b) devote much of those discretionary resources to the formulation and accomplishment of specific, attainable, measurable, and highly visible goals. That process usually can be described by this sequence: The new pastor arrives and earns the trust and confidence of the people by accepting and fulfilling the obligation to pay the rent. Concurrently the new pastor is identifying three to ten potential allies who will actively participate in the formulation of those ministry goals and in mobilizing the support required to attain them. Frequently, one or more of those goals are unfulfilled dreams shared by several of those allies.

One or more may be largely the creation of that new pastor. Others are children with several parents.

TWO CRUCIAL DISTINCTIONS

The pastor who concentrates on paying the rent often will define the workload for the coming week in terms of tasks and relationships. "Monday morning the number-one pillar in this congregation has surgery scheduled for eight o'clock, which means I will have to be at the hospital with the family from about seven until noon. Tuesday afternoon I have the funeral for a teenager killed in an automobile accident Saturday night, and I have to spend time with the family. Wednesday evening we have our first Lenten service of the year. A term paper I am working on in my class for the Doctor of Ministry degree is due next Monday, so I must get it in the mail Friday. I have two marriage counseling sessions scheduled for the middle of the week, and several months ago I promised the Home-builders Sunday school class that I would teach a six-week study of the book of Mark beginning next Sunday. Saturday morning is a critical meeting of a denominational committee I chair, and I cannot be late for that. I also have a wedding scheduled for late Saturday afternoon, and I am obligated to go to the reception and dinner afterward. The work of a parish pastor is never finished."

By contrast, the goal-driven pastor follows a different rule book that affirms the fact that paying the rent will require one-half to three-quarters of the hours in the coming week, but thinks in a different conceptual framework in scheduling the workload and deciding how that discretionary time will be used. "Our number-one goal has been to reach younger families with children at home. One of the means-to-an-end components of that effort is to acquire the property next door, raze the buildings, expand our off-street parking, and construct a new wing to house an expansion of our children's ministries. The congregational meeting to approve the capital funds campaign is three weeks away, and Harold Smith is the only person with any influence here who has voiced serious reservations. I must get together with Harold and see if we can identify his real reasons for not supporting it. While we can live with some abstentions from voting, ideally everyone casting a vote at that congregational meeting will favor going ahead. I hope I can persuade Harold to support it, but at a minimum not to come out in open opposition. In addition, Terry Campbell and Pat Keller have both indicated they would like to see an expansion of our ministries with very young children. I have to set up an appointment with the two of them together to see if they want to accept major leadership responsibilities in this or whether they only want to help make it happen. In September, as a part of that larger goal of reaching young families and younger childless couples, we are scheduled to begin our new Saturday evening worship service. That is only six months away, and we still have only three volunteers committed to serve as the worship team for that service. We need at least four more, and I would prefer a total of ten. We are determined to double our worship attendance over the next seven years; what will that require in terms of additional program staff? Should I work with our personnel committee in defining those needs? Or should we create a special single-purpose task force to study that issue?"

In addition to paying the rent, these goal-driven pastors also accept the responsibility to serve as agents of planned change initiated from within that organization.[4] Instead of conceptualizing tasks as part of the responsibility for paying the rent, the goal-driven pastor uses that discretionary time to (a) enlist allies to help formulate and implement missional goals and (b) accomplish the tasks required for fulfillment of those goals.

WHAT'S THE DIFFERENCE?

Calling on a parishioner who is in the hospital, attending a committee meeting, officiating at the wedding of a member, leading worship, teaching an adult Sunday school class for six weeks, preparing and delivering inspirational sermons, and working with the finance committee on the preparation of a budget for the coming year are all important pastoral activities. They are tasks that represent paying the rent.

In contrast, a goal is an end to be achieved. By definition, it will be specific, attainable, and measurable. A goal is not the same as a dream. A common dream is, "I would like to see our church reverse the numerical decline of recent years and double in size." A goal would define the constituency to be reached, identify the changes required to reach and serve that constituency, and state the tasks needed to make all of that happen. To grow younger in the median age of the membership is a dream. To design and implement ministries with young adults ages twenty-three to twenty-eight is a goal. To create, staff, and schedule a Saturday evening worship service designed for that age cohort is a task that should be only one component of the larger strategy to attain that goal.

Completion of the tasks required to pay the rent dominates the thinking of the pastor who is content with a maintenance ministry and/or who wants to direct those discretionary resources to a personal agenda. In these congregations, the local rule book places a high priority on perpetuating local traditions, care of the members, and maintenance of the real estate.

Paying the rent is a priority for the goal-driven pastor, but the fulfilling challenge is in directing that discretionary time and energy toward building alliances for change and designing the strategy required to attain the appropriate goals.

A reasonably competent task-driven pastor who accepts the responsibility to pay the rent fully and on time usually is able

120

to maintain a congregation on a plateau in size. While the pastor faces changes in that passing parade of parishioners, the newcomers will equal in number those who depart by death, dropping out, switching churches, or moving away.

In at least three out of five congregations, the newly arrived pastor who (a) accepts and affirms the importance of fully paying the rent and on time; (b) settles in with the expectation that this will be at least a ten to thirty-year pastorate; (c) recognizes and accepts the need to revise the local rule book before or concurrently with the introduction of innovative practices; (d) allocates most of those discretionary resources to identifying, enlisting, and motivating allies; and (e) leads those alliances in the formulation and implementation of new ministry goals can enjoy a doubling in the worship attendance every seven to ten years.

The downside is that the task-driven approach to ministry rarely is appropriate in congregations averaging more than 350 at worship. All too often the task-driven approach has turned out to be an effective means of shrinking the congregation averaging 400 or more at worship down to fewer than 350.

The downside to the goal-driven style is that it rarely is appropriate in congregations averaging more than 700 at worship.

GOALS OR POTENTIAL?

This introduces the second of these two crucial distinctions in ministerial leadership. This is the huge difference between the result when the pastor builds an alliance that formulates and implements clearly attainable goals and when the pastor brings a vision-driven approach to ministry that is based, not simply on formulating and attaining goals, but on identifying and fulfilling the potential within that worshiping community.

Most efforts to secure broad-based support for specific

attainable and measurable goals tend to underestimate the potential within that congregation. The compromises required to secure that broad base of congregational support usually are in adoption of less ambitious and less challenging goals.

The long-range planning committee consisting of twenty-five members representing every faction, generation, class, organization, standing committee, group, and social network within that congregation usually can reach a consensus on one or more specific, attainable, and measurable goals. The compromises required to build that consensus, however, frequently mean "watering down" specific proposals to modest levels so everyone can agree that is an attainable goal.

For the goal-driven pastor, two of the key words are *alliance* and *attainable*.

By contrast, the challenge to identify and fulfill the potential for a more extensive ministry usually comes from either (1) the pastor or (2) the pastor and two to six like-minded visionary volunteer allies.

For the goal-driven pastor, two of the key words are *alliance* and *attainable*. Ideally that alliance will include a majority of the most widely respected and influential volunteer leaders. By contrast, the vision-driven leader replaces *attainable* with *potential*, thus raising the ceiling on what is perceived to be possible. That vision-driven leader also is looking for a much smaller number of allies, with the key criterion being vision rather than numbers. The vision-driven leader is comfortable and, hopefully, competent in challenging the people to do what they all know cannot be done. Instead of helping the congregation formulate and attain its goals, this style of ministerial leadership focuses on challenging the people to fulfill their God-given potential. The former lives under self-imposed ceilings. The latter believes ceilings should be perceived as challenges, not as barriers. That distinction introduces the differences between the third group of pastors, the goal-driven ministers, and an even smaller fourth cadre, those who are driven by a vision of a new tomorrow.

AN IDEOLOGICAL ISSUE

At this point the reader should be advised of a deep ideological chasm ahead. The contemporary ecclesiastical culture in the United States is heavily committed ideologically to the democratic notion that the voices of the people should be heard and heeded, that the best goals enjoy a broad base of local ownership, and that the ideal style of pastoral leadership focuses on helping a congregation formulate, adopt, and implement its goals. A persuasive case can be made that is an excellent approach to ministry in congregations averaging between 85 and 300 at worship.

A persuasive case also can be made that this is why there are so few very large congregations in American Protestantism! The basic generalization is that the larger the size of the congregation and/or the faster the numerical growth rate, the more

These vision-driven pastors, who also affirm the value of specific goals but see them as building blocks for turning that vision into reality, constitute the fourth and smallest group of contemporary parish pastors. That paucity helps to explain why there are so few large Protestant congregations in North America.

likely that congregation has enjoyed the leadership of a long-tenured vision-driven pastor rather than the goal-driven minister who excelled at building broad-based alliances that formulated the goals.

The ideological division in the ecclesiastical culture finds on one side those who contend that the senior pastor should be a leader among leaders and those who affirm the value of the pastor who accepts and fulfills the role of the "transformational" leader.

These vision-driven pastors, who also affirm the value of specific goals but see them as building blocks for turning that vision into reality, constitute the fourth and smallest group of contemporary parish pastors. That paucity helps to explain why there are so few large Protestant congregations in North America.

Another rarely mentioned, but extremely valuable, quality of the best of the vision-driven pastors is that they understand and affirm the importance of the rent's being paid. But they see their role as making sure it is paid, usually by other paid staff members and/or volunteers, rather than feeling that they must make all of those payments personally.

The downside of this scenario is that a significant number become victims when they attempt to cast a challenging vision before a small congregation in which the leaders limit their evaluation to only one question: Is the rent being paid in full and on time? That is the page in the local rule book people often emphasize.

Another subtle characteristic of the congregation led by a vision-driven, entrepreneurial pastor who identifies as mere challenges what others see as ceilings is in the volunteer lay leadership attracted to these churches. These very large congregations tend to attract more than their share of laypersons who are more comfortable with an abundance, rather than a scarcity-driven approach to planning. They also appreciate the entrepreneurial gifts of that vision-driven pastor. Most important of all, they are convinced that the Christian faith is a transformational religion. For many, this conviction is based on their personal experience as they reflect on how their own life was transformed when they became active disciples of Jesus Christ. Some carry this discussion an additional step as they point out that the transformational power of Christianity is a predictable consequence of its being a religion that projects high expectations of anyone who commits to being a disciple of Jesus Christ. Therefore, they argue that by definition a Christian congregation cannot fulfill its calling by operating with a maintenance approach to ministry. It must project high expectations of both individual members and of itself as a worshiping community. Therefore, they gratefully and unreservedly support the vision-driven pastor who challenges people to do what they know they cannot do.

THE PROBLEM OF SUCCESSION

When the first four of these five factors—path dependency, a hostile ecclesiastical culture, low expectations, and a scarcity system of governance—are combined, that helps to explain the shortage of vision-driven ministerial leaders. That also helps to explain why a disproportionately large number of the very large churches of today were founded after 1970. It is relatively easy to find a vision-driven pastor who will plant what will quickly become a very large congregation. It is somewhat more difficult to find a successor who also is a vision-driven leader.

A saying of World War II was, "There are many old pilots. There also are many bold pilots, but there are few old, bold pilots." Likewise, there exists a huge inventory of old congregations that trace their history back for more than a century. There also are many congregations that have enjoyed the leadership of a vision-driven pastor, but there are few that have enjoyed the leadership of five consecutive vision-driven senior ministers!

When another factor is added to that formula, it also helps to explain why relatively few congregations affiliated with the mainline Protestant denominations average more than 800 at worship. Sometime during the early to mid-1960s, most of these denominations cut back sharply on the new churches that were organized each year. The very large congregation founded in the 1970s may not have had to face the issue of succession yet. The very large congregation founded in the 1950s probably has had to search for one or more successors to that vision-driven minister who was the founding pastor. Some have enjoyed the two-in-a-row or three-in-a-row success in that search, but far more replaced the vision-driven leader with a pastor who concentrated only on paying the rent.

Perhaps the most subtle variable in the succession issue can be summarized in the old adage, "Don't fix what ain't broke!" The congregation that has enjoyed many years of effective leadership from a vision-driven pastor often will look for a successor who will seek to perpetuate that same ministry plan. Sometimes that is appropriate. Frequently, however, the time has come to challenge a new cadre of volunteer leaders with a new vision for a new era. Frequently, this is a product of a changing context. The "Old First Church Downtown" congregation of today serves in a radically different urban environment than it did in the 1950s, when it may have been the denominational flagship congregation in that county or perhaps in the whole state. The university church of the 1990s serves in a different context than it enjoyed in the 1950s. The farming community church of 1955 now serves in a community in which retirees, people employed in tourism and recreation, and those who accept a thirty-mile commute to a city paycheck in exchange for country living now outnumber farmers by a five-to-one ratio.

In many other congregations the time has come to identify a new constituency. The church pillars of the 1950s are disappearing to be replaced by younger generations with different agendas and new expectations.

When that long-tenured vision-driven pastor retires or resigns, the temptation often is to seek a successor who will be a younger version of that beloved minister. The dream is for continuity with the past, not for a new vision for a new era. A common result is to look for a successor who will be able to perpetuate the past, rather than someone who will challenge the people with a new vision. Tradition replaces vision as a powerful influence in policy formation.

One result often is that the "unintentional" interim pastor, who concludes that the conflict in expectations is unacceptable, departs after two or three years. Another is that what once was a very large congregation averaging over 800 at worship drops into the 400 to 700 average attendance bracket.

THE KINGDOM BUILDERS

The goal-driven and the vision-driven pastors share several common characteristics. Both groups of ministers accept the responsibility that goes with serving as an initiating leader. By contrast, the task-driven pastor tends to react to the initiatives of others.

Most of the goal-driven and vision-driven pastors also affirm the importance of core values. These core values are fully internalized. Too often core values, like mission statements, are superficial expressions of pious rhetoric that have not been internalized by either the pastor or the leaders of that congregation. Slogans can be useful in rallying people in support of a specific task or goal. Having capital funds campaigns and enlisting volunteers to construct a house for a low-income family under the auspices of Habitat For Humanity are two examples of the practical usefulness of slogans. Slogans can be used to express core values, but slogans are not the same as core values.

A third common characteristic is that both can be classified as congregation-building leaders. They are not maintenance pastors. They operate on the assumption that their congregation is called to reach more people with the good news of Jesus Christ. They accept the fact that in today's culture, that requires an emphasis on relevance, quality, innovation, choices, and persistence.

Too often core values, like mission statements, are superficial expressions of pious rhetoric that have not been internalized by either the pastor or the leaders of that congregation.

Those characteristics introduce the fifth and the smallest group of pastors. With one big exception, they resemble the vision-driven pastors described here. That big exception is that their primary focus is not on congregation building, but rather on helping to build the kingdom of God.

This can be illustrated by the way one of them conceptualizes the workload of the next few weeks. "Ken Johnson, who has been on our staff for five years, has left to plant a new mission in a community fifteen miles to the west. We need to replace Ken with an experienced pastor who has the potential to become an effective church planter. So far, none of the people we have contacted have responded with promising suggestions. We need to intensify that search process. In each of the past three summers, we have sent teams of ten to fifteen adults to help our missionaries in Peru plant new missions. We have another team set to go this summer, but I wonder if we are overloading that missionary couple. Perhaps we should look for a different mission field to which we will send a church-planting team next year? Four of our members who are bivocational ministers serving small rural churches north of here will be moving away this summer. We really need to strength-en our program of enlisting and training members to serve as bivocational pastors. We now have fourteen who serve con-gregations, and we should be able to expand that to at least twenty, so we could staff more of these small congregations. We now offer two teaching events a year for leaders from other congregations who want to come and learn from our experiences. The demand is there for us to offer more. We probably should go to three next year and four the following year. The drug problem among the high school kids is getting worse, and it is unfair to expect the public school officials to solve it by themselves. I talked with the mayor about this last month, and he said he was working on a city-wide citizens' committee to address this issue. Maybe I need to make an appointment to see if I can nudge him to move a little faster. The pastor of the Latino congregation that meets in our building told me yesterday he is convinced they won't realize their growth potential as long as they meet in the building of an Anglo church. Maybe we need to help them find a meeting place they can call their own."

Many of the congregations averaging more than 2,500 at worship have evolved from a self-defined congregation-build-ing identity to a kingdom-building role, thanks to the leader-ship of a kingdom-building pastor.

While it was mentioned earlier, a fifth part of the explana-tion for the small number of very large churches merits a few additional observations.

SUCCESSION

The greatest point of institutional vulnerability among the very large congregations is in ministerial succession. When the vision-driven pastor who feels called to the kingdom-building role departs and is followed by a goal-driven minis-ter, the usual result is a plateau in size followed by the threat

129

of a potential shrinkage in numbers. This evokes pleas that "We need to take better care of our members." That produces a radically different set of priorities in the allocation of scarce resources from challenging people to do what they know they cannot do.

When either the goal-driven pastor or the vision-driven minister departs and is followed by a pastor who concentrates on paying the rent promptly and in full, the usual result is (a) a gradual numerical decline as losses are only partially offset by newcomers; (b) bewilderment ("I'm a highly competent minister and I pay the rent in full every week; why are the numbers going down?"); and (c) considerable, but less than universal, contentment by the members, many of whom felt they were challenged beyond their ability to respond, the pace was too fast, congregational life was becoming excessively complex, the "strange face syndrome" made the long-tenured members become lost in a sea of anonymity—and all they really want is a church served by a pastor who pays the rent promptly.

When the vision-driven or the goal-driven pastor leaves and is followed by a task-oriented minister who combines dull preaching, an introverted personality, and a low level of productivity, the first response often is a plea to increase the number of paid staff. Concurrently there is an acceleration in the rate of departure of the constituency.

Finally, in a relatively small number of very large congregations, the highly effective, vision-driven pastor is followed by another reasonably competent and vision-driven minister, but it soon becomes apparent that this is a serious mismatch. The new minister comes with a substantially different belief system or a completely different vision of what God is calling this congregation to be or a set of professional skills that match the culture and needs of a completely different cohort in the population or without the level of skill in building interpersonal relationships that is required to bridge that transition period following the departure of that personable visionary.

WHAT DO THE PEOPLE WANT?

Perhaps the most widely and openly discussed barrier to the emergence of more very large congregations is attitudinal. Most of the current members of most congregations in American Protestantism do not want the anonymity, complexity, and discontinuity that are inherent components of the big church. They want continuity with the past, intimacy, simplicity, the perpetuation of local traditions, predictability, and the control that are valued characteristics of smaller congregations.

Therefore, it is rare, but not surprising, to find that relatively few congregations that were founded before 1970 and have never exceeded an annual average worship attendance of 150 are eager to make the changes required to grow into a very large church. They are comfortable with the rule book they have been following for decades and display little interest in mastering a new rule book for a new game on a new playing field.

A common illustration is the congregation that has been averaging between 85 and 135 at worship for the past forty years. The population of that community has increased fourfold over those four decades, and that means a new playing field. The potential for numerical growth is present, but the average worship attendance in this church has dropped from 125 ten years ago to 115 last year. The changes required to learn a new game to reach a new constituency and more people exceed the degree of change the people find acceptable.

STAFFING

Another set of barriers to the emergence of more very large congregations can be identified under the broad umbrella of paid staff. Six stand out here. The first is the change in the role of the senior pastor who was trained to do ministry. The new role requires the senior minister to focus on making sure ministry is being done, rather than on doing it.

A second is in staff relationships. The "hub-and-spoke" model in which every paid program staff member (plus frequently the administrative assistant and the part-time business administrator) is directly accountable to the pastor often is a workable configuration in the congregation averaging 200 to 700 at worship. It is much less likely to be the appropriate configuration for the very large congregation where trust and delegation are crucial components of staff relationships. To grow beyond 700 in average worship attendance usually requires a new rule book for a new staff configuration.

Third, as size goes up, new criteria are introduced into the process of selecting program staff members. One facet is the shift from "doing it" to "making it happen." More important is the shift from staffing to perpetuate yesterday to staffing to create new tomorrows.

Fourth is the change from designing the staff configuration to reflect staff specialties (Christian education, music, youth ministries, evangelism, pastoral care, administration, etc.) to a new focus on staffing the distinctive identity of that congregation. Thus the self-identified congregation of congregations will not utilize the same staff configuration as the self-identified congregation of communities. (See point 9 of chapter 7 for an elaboration of this distinction.)

Fifth is the changing definition of the word *team*. It may be appropriate and productive for the paid program staff in the congregation averaging 350-600 to conceptualize themselves as a team. The senior minister or the executive pastor usually is the captain of that team.

In the very large congregation, however, a better model may be to conceptualize the paid program staff and the heavily involved lay volunteers as a team of teams. Many, frequently most, of the members of these ministry teams are lay volunteers. The line of demarcation between the part-time

132

paid staff member and the volunteer may be in skill, not in hours invested in the average workweek. A typical team may include five to fifteen volunteers, one full-time paid staffer, one to five part-time paid persons, and its own custom-designed rule book.

Finally, and perhaps most important, is the training and preparation of paid staff members. For the nineteen out of twenty Protestant congregations averaging fewer than 500 at worship, the usual assumption is that ideally all program staff members will have had professional training for ministry in a theological school, Bible college, or university. In many traditions a seminary degree still is a requirement for ordination.

In an increasing proportion of the very large Protestant churches, however, the most valued qualities of potential future staff members are (1) good character; (2) a deep Christian commitment; (3) a sympathetic and supportive understanding of the culture, core values, and distinctive mission of this particular congregation; (4) an earned level of trust by the policy makers of both paid staff and volunteer leaders; (5) a high level of competence in one or more areas of ministry; (6) a clear sense of a call to ministry; (7) an openness to advanced in-service training to enhance that level of competence; (8) an above-average level of competence in interpersonal relationships; and (9) a record as an effective volunteer in ministry in that congregation. Academic and professional credentials are tied for tenth place in the chapter on staffing in that rule book.

In other words, staffing with outsiders may be the appropriate strategy for smaller congregations; the very large churches increasingly are turning to finding staff from within the membership.

START SMALL

While this syndrome is now becoming ancient history, the effects are still being felt. This barrier was most common in the 1945–80 era, when a common strategy was to use a small-church model in planting new missions. This called for bringing together a cadre of laypersons for that new mission. A pastor was assigned to lead that venture. Frequently the pastor's experience did not include service on the staff of a very large church, but was limited to congregations averaging fewer than 150 at worship. This model was based on the value of one-to-one relationships with the mission developer at the hub of that network. That model tended to attract people who preferred a small congregation based on intimacy, a close personal relationship with the pastor, one worship service every weekend, the absence of anonymity, strong lay control over policy making, and a high degree of predictability. The hope was that out of acorns mighty oak trees would grow. The reality was that the vast majority of these new missions (1) closed before their tenth birthday, (2) merged into another congregation, or (3) plateaued in size with an average worship attendance under 150.

In other words, the strategy of using a small-church model for new missions became a barrier to the emergence of more very large churches.

In recent years an increasing proportion of new missions have been designed on the basis of a large-church model. A common goal is that the first public worship service will include at least 500 attendees and the average attendance for the first year will be at least 350 and will exceed 700 by year seven.

IS REAL ESTATE THE BARRIER?

While many congregational leaders place the limitations of real estate as one of the two or three most influential reasons for the current shortage of very large churches, it is placed next to last here for several reasons. First, it is highly subjective. If the leaders are convinced that the limitations are the major barrier to reaching more people with the good news of Jesus Christ, then it is a huge barrier. If the leaders do not identify this as a major barrier, it usually becomes a minor issue.

Second, real estate probably will become a more influential factor in the twenty-first century than it was in the twentieth. Third, because it is so easy to provide tangible measurements of real estate (in contrast to the difficulty of providing equally tangible measurements of competence, enthusiasm, vision, tradition, leadership, and "our constituency"), it is tempting to focus on the problems of space.

The fourth, and perhaps the most subtle, variable is the absence of agreement on criteria. How much land does a congregation need to be able to accommodate 800 to 1,200 people at worship on the typical weekend? The only clear answer is, It depends. If the year is 1955, the answer may be three acres. If it is 1975, the answer may be five acres. If it is 2010, the answer is more likely to be ten or more acres. If the question is raised on the Atlantic seaboard or in California, the answer is more likely to be a smaller number than in the Midwest or the south-central states.

If the schedule calls for seven different worship services on the weekend, the answer will be a smaller number than if the goal is a thousand people in one worship service.

If the local culture requires 500 private motor vehicles to bring 1,000 people to church on Sunday morning, that number will be much larger than if most of the worshipers use public transportation to come to church or if most walk.

If the expectation is that this congregation could, should, and will triple in size at this site, the size of land needed obviously will be much larger than if the goal is to plateau at a thousand in average worship attendance.

The **big** variable, however, in answering that question on land lies in the definition of a "full-service church." If that definition includes worship, Sunday school, a modest weekday ministry, and a tradition-driven statement of purpose, then one acre per 100 people at worship probably will be adequate.

If, however, the definition of a "full-service church" includes worship; a variety of learning opportunities for all ages; an extensive indoor and outdoor recreation program; a Christian day school for ages 3 through 12; an extensive camping ministry; a retirement village; acceptance of a role as a teaching church; a full ministry with death, including a funeral home, cemetery, and a columbarium; a distance learning center for adult education; a retreat center; perhaps a hospice; an average worship attendance of at least 4,500; and one or two other specialized ministries, then this probably will require 120 to 400 acres of land.

In other words, how much land is required for the very large congregation? The answer is, Enough to accommodate the dream.

That also explains why there are so few very large congregations in American Protestantism today. The potential is greater than most dreams.

Finally, one of the most powerful forces in opposition to the emergence of more very large congregations is the widespread reliance on rule books, both congregational and denominational, that are filled with obsolete, internally inconsistent, and counterproductive rules on how to do church. They were written in a different era for a different constituency and for use on a different playing field. Many of those rules were written by white males of a Western European ancestry who dropped out of the game when they relocated their place of residence to a cemetery, but who still control how the game will be played.

CHAPTER FIVE

Leadership Roles

"C urrently I'm in the third year of my fifth pastorate," explained the Reverend Don Johnson, the 55-year-old senior minister of a congregation averaging over 1,500 in weekly worship attendance. The occasion was a luncheon for a national gathering of senior pastors, and the minister seated to Don's left had initiated this get-acquainted conversation between two strangers from two different religious traditions.

"In my first pastorate, I graduated from seminary on a Friday, and a week from the following Sunday I was preaching to about fifty people in an open country church in the Midwest," continued Don. "For the previous several years, this congregation had been served by a minister who also served a larger church in a town six miles away. In recent years that church had begun to grow as the larger community slowly became exurban in character. It reached the point where it wanted, needed, and could afford a full-time minister. My predecessor, along with a couple of denominational staff, urged the people in the open country church to close and go into town to church. They rejected that and decided a better alternative would be to raise enough money to seek their own full-time minister for at least a year or two. I arrived in early June, and that summer we had between thirty and sixty in worship. Their tradition had been to close for the first two Sundays in August to give the minister a vacation. I broke that tradition, but they were the two low-attendance Sundays of the summer.

"My role turned out to be a combination of shepherd, cheerleader, evangelist, and preacher. During that first year, I called at nearly every home within five or six miles as we expanded the definition of our service area. More important, perhaps, I was the enthusiastic cheerleader. We celebrated every victory, no matter how tiny. Gradually we were able to replace the institutional survival emphasis I was given when I arrived with a more positive self-image. Two young mothers helped me organize a children's choir, and a grandmother directed it. That was a powerful symbol for a congregation that had been told repeatedly it was a dying church. By the end of my fourth year, church attendance was averaging 150 and morale was high. Shortly after the beginning of my fifth year, nine of the fifteen people elected to serve on the church council had joined during the previous four years. What was even more impressive to me was that no one commented on that until after I had pointed it out. I felt that for a city boy born and reared in Philadelphia, I had completed a successful post-seminary apprenticeship."

"That sounds to me like a remarkably effective first-pastorate-out-of-seminary performance," affirmed the luncheon companion. "What did you do next?"

"My second pastorate also lasted approximately five years," recalled Don, "but it called for a different leadership role. My new role was to challenge a comfortable congregation to do what the people knew not only could not be done, but probably should not even be attempted. The highly visible example of this came when I challenged the people to accept the fact that this really was a big church and the time had come to see ourselves as a congregation of congregations, rather than simply as a church of 175 members. The test came when we created a special task force that recommended we expand the Sunday morning schedule from Sunday school followed by worship to worship followed by Sunday school followed by a second worship service. The critics contended that would split the church, destroy the feeling of being one big family, violate the local rule book, overwork the adult choir, which would have to sing at both services, and undermine the Sunday school and that too few people would come to an 8:30 Sunday morning service to make it a meaningful experience. Less visible and much less controversial was what I believe was more important. That was the challenge to expand the weekday and weeknight ministries and to focus on expanding the group life. The response to that was overwhelmingly positive, and by the end of my third year more than 40 percent of our adults were engaged in small groups that met weekly. During my fourth year we added a Saturday evening service to the schedule. A year later the combined attendance of the three services averaged nearly 350."

"Your story of your second pastorate coincides with my experience," commented the luncheon companion. "When people are properly challenged, they respond. What happened next?"

"My third pastorate covered eleven years and required me to learn and practice a new leadership role. I thought I had been reasonably effective in evoking positive responses to serious challenges, but in this situation I encountered a force that I did not fully understand until later. This is the powerful attachment people have to place. One example is that most people sit in the same place at the family dining table. Another is that they sit in the same place in church, they park their car in the same space if they can, and they sleep on the same side of the bed. People place a high value on continuity, stability, and predictability.

"In this, my third pastorate, I found myself in a situation where it was clear to me that this congregation must relocate to a larger site and build new and larger facilities. We were meeting in a functionally obsolete building on a two-acre site at a good location on a state highway, but the owner of the adjacent property would not sell us more land. I challenged the people to consider relocating. The response was a proposal to construct a classroom-office addition to the old building. Despite my reservations, we built the addition to that sacred place with practically no opposition.

"A few days after we moved into the new building, a long-time friend came by and, as we talked about my experience, explained the differences between the leader who challenges people to do what they know they cannot do and the visionary leader who overcomes objections to radical change by communicating a new vision of a new and different tomorrow and wins support for that vision. That was the day I changed my leadership role from challenger to visionary."

"What's the difference?" questioned the listening acquaintance.

"There are at least five big differences," answered this reflective pastor. "The first is the difference between continuity with the past and discontinuity. Normally, leaders challenge people to keep on doing what they have been doing, only better or more of it. The football coach challenges the players to win more games than they won last year. A parent challenges a child to earn better grades in school. We challenged our people with the need for more space, and they responded that if we can maintain continuity with the past, they will meet that challenge.

"A vision for a new tomorrow usually is based on a high degree of discontinuity with the past. The factory worker who dropped out of high school for a high-paying job holds before his children the vision of graduating from college. The homemaker returns to school when the youngest child leaves home to undergird a vision of a new tomorrow. The tenured professor resigns to start a new business. In our case we made the mistake of challenging our people with the need for more meeting rooms. They accepted the challenge, and we had a very successful building program that was all paid for two years after completion. My mistake, and as the leader of that congregation it was my mistake, was that I should have held up a vision of what God was calling this congregation to become in the years ahead. I let the means-to-an-end issue become the driving force. That driving force should have been a compelling vision of a new tomorrow.

"A second difference is between the focus on specific, attainable, and measurable goals and an emphasis on fulfilling the potential. In that first pastorate out of seminary, we organized around attainable goals and we celebrated every victory, no matter how tiny it was. That was an appropriate strategy for the cheerleader trying to strengthen the self-image of a congregation that was focused on institutional survival. By contrast, most of the people at this luncheon are the senior pastors of very large churches where the emphasis should be on identifying and fulfilling the potential. Goals tend to evolve into ceilings. Visions have a floor but no ceiling.

"A third, and perhaps the biggest, difference in the churches is the distinction between what I, as a sinful human being, can do and what God can do. We challenge people with goals that emerge out of the deliberations of a task force or that one person articulates. The visionary leader paints a picture of what the Lord is calling the church to be and to do. We also have a book

"The visionary leader does not have the time required to build broad-based support. The challenger seeks broad-based support for 'our goal.' The visionary leader seeks allies who are driven by what they see as a call from God."

that we can use to document the content of that vision.

"A fourth difference is the challenger usually can work within the limitations of the local rule book. The visionary leader, however, almost always has to either ignore that local rule book or introduce a radical revision of it.

"A fifth difference is the support base. The challenging role for a pastor is consistent with the goal of broad-based support. The ideal is 100 percent of the people will accept the challenge and join together in meeting it. When that relatively new church building is destroyed by a fire or a tornado, the challenge may be to rebuild on that site, and nearly every member becomes an active supporter of that goal. When the obsolete building on an inadequate site at what is now a poor location is destroyed by fire, the visionary leader holds up the dream of new facilities on a larger site at a better location designed to reach new generations of people. That visionary leader is not looking for a broad base of support for what probably is a controversial recommendation. All the visionary leader needs is the enthusiastic support of seven to thirty widely respected, future-oriented, influential, and competent volunteer leaders who become active allies in enlisting support for that compelling vision. The visionary leader does not have the time required to build broad-based support. The challenger seeks broad-based support for 'our goal.' The visionary leader seeks allies who are driven by what they see as a call from God."

"So what did you do when you accepted the role of the visionary leader?" came the question.

"First of all, I encouraged our people to celebrate the completion of the building program as evidence that this congregation could do whatever we decided we should be doing. However, I always added the reservation that this was but one step in a long journey, not the end of the road. About a year after we moved into the new addition, most of our people gradually became aware of the need for more parking, for more space for worship, for a bigger fellowship hall, and for a larger narthex. I quietly fed the fires of discontent. Ever since the second year of my first pastorate, I use the first Sunday of January for what I call my state of the church sermon. Twenty-eight months after we moved into the new addition, I lifted up the vision of what I believed God was calling this congregation to become and to be doing as a pioneer in ministry. I emphasized that larger facilities at a better location and a larger site were merely means-to-an-end issues. It took three years to sell that vision, another year to find and agree on a good relocation site, a year for planning and financing, another year for construction, and a year to get used to meeting in new facilities at a new location. Those seven years were the most stressful of my whole ministry!"

"That's three pastorates in approximately twenty-two years," summarized the luncheon partner. "Where are you now?"

"My fourth pastorate also placed me in a building situation," replied Don, "but this time the need was to build the ministry staff. This also required learning new leadership roles and styles as well as learning how to operate with a new rule book. In seminary and in that first pastorate I was taught to do it. Whatever the assignment was, I did it and was evaluated on how well I fulfilled the assignment. That included writing term papers, attending class, visiting people in the hospital, preaching, officiating at funerals, leading worship, answering the mail, or enlisting new members. My responsibility was to do it.

"In my third pastorate, the one I just described, I gradually began to learn how to work with staff. At first, I used the hub-and-spoke model, which calls for everyone to report to and be accountable to one leader. That was compatible with the role I had accepted as the pastor-in-charge. The buck stopped with me. That also was what satisfied the lay leadership. They agreed the pastor should be responsible for what the paid staff did or did not do.

"About halfway through that third pastorate I began to recognize that one of the price tags on relocation to a much larger site would be paid for, at least in part, out of the salaries we would not pay the program staff we would need,

143

but could not afford to hire. That is what happened, and that was one reason why those last seven years were so stressful. At that point we had a full-time associate minister who was a generalist and who had spent his previous twelve years serving small churches, a full-time director of Christian education who also really was a generalist in that field, and a part-time, semiretired minister who preached three or four times a year but concentrated on pastoral care. I conceptualized the staff configuration as consisting of two overlapping teams. One was our four-person program staff team. The other included both the program staff and the five-person support staff, three of whom were part-time. Everyone agreed I was the captain of both teams.

"When I began my fourth pastorate, I expected to perpetuate that model," continued Don, "but I soon realized that building a new staff also gave me the freedom to design a new staff configuration for a new playing field and to create a new rule book on staff roles and relationships. I also learned that building a new staff is a more challenging and difficult assignment than constructing a new building."

"Tell me about the configuration you chose," interrupted the impatient luncheon companion.

"At that time the literature in the field of leadership stressed the goal of a flat organizational structure, rather than a hierarchical model, and the value of teams. So I began with the dream of a seven-person program staff team and two teams of support staff. One of these would be responsible for the real estate, and one would support the program staff. I planned for the Executive Pastor to head the two support teams, and I would be the captain of the program staff team."

"How did that work?" inquired another person at the table who had been a passive listener to this point.

"It was a satisfactory model for a couple of years, but in retrospect I can see four reasons why it turned out to be the wrong model for us," explained Don.

"First, we outgrew it. It probably was an appropriate model for a congregation averaging 500 to 700 at worship, but when we passsed the 800 mark, I began to realize it was not the right model for us.

"Second, it consumed too much of my time and energy. I had too many responsibilities. It may be that what we called a team really was a nice name for that old hub-and-spoke model. We changed the name but not the internal dynamics, and we stuck with the old rule book.

"Third, we were fortunate in being able to find several exceptionally competent and experienced program specialists from among our membership.

"We discovered we had scores of members who had an exceptionally high level of competence in a specialized area. One was a woman who had pioneered the introduction into the public schools of parenting classes for adults with children ages birth to three years. Another was a man who worked full-time on the production of videotapes for educational purposes. A third was a man who had just retired as the psychologist on the staff of a medical clinic. A fourth was a woman who had specialized for twenty years as a consultant to corporations converting to the system of worker teams. A fifth was a husband-wife couple in their late fifties who had designed, partly as a hobby for themselves, a highly structured weekend retreat designed for newly engaged couples. They had staffed these retreats, which were sponsored by churches, in at least thirty states over the past several years.

"Today, all but four of our part-time and full-time paid program staff members are people we enlisted from our own membership. We replaced the generalists, who had been hired from the outside, with specialists who really were top-flight professionals and who knew and were supportive of our unique congregational culture. We had moved from trying to train generalists, who really should have been in smaller congregations, in how to be professionals on the staff of a very large congregation to bringing in experienced and highly skilled specialists from among people who understood the characteristics of the very large church.

"Fourth—and this took me a long time to grasp—we really were attempting to perpetuate the small-church concepts I had enjoyed so much in my first pastorate. A church should hire people to do ministry. So, as the workload grows, the paid staff is enlarged. The professionals we brought in conceptualized their role as challenging laity to exercise their gifts as members of volunteer-paid staff teams."

"I'm not sure I understand what you're telling us," inquired a fourth person at the table who was obviously captivated by the conversation when it turned to staffing.

"Since we're about out of time here, let me describe my present situation," offered Dan. "In this, the third year of my fifth pastorate, I am trying to put together what I've learned about my responsibilities as a leader. As I said earlier, my first distinctive role was to be the cheerleader for what had been identified as a dying church. The next was to challenge the people, in a contented congregation that was threatened by complacency, with the limits imposed by continuity with the past. The third was to become a visionary leader. The fourth was to build three teams of paid staff who accepted the responsibility for doing ministry. I accepted the responsibility for leading those teams, and therefore I simply assumed that supervision and control were two of the givens in that definition of leadership. Currently my number-one leadership responsibility in what is a megachurch is to create and support an environment for highly skilled specialists. They don't need, or want, supervision. They require support, information about the larger picture, and protection when someone objects to a new ministry. To use the football analogy, I now spend more time as a blocking back than I do as the quarterback. The quarterback role was consistent with the role I accepted when I challenged people to do what they knew they could not do. I also spend more time and energy on improving and enhancing the culture of the congregation than I devote to controlling the work of the paid staff. Occasionally I must accept the role of mentor or coach or motivator, but that is largely with new part-time program staff."

"How would you describe your present staff configuration?" asked one of the listeners.

"We are a team of teams," came the quick reply. "We now have twelve ministry teams. Each one is composed of one to four part-time paid specialists, a full-time staff person, and three to fifteen volunteers. We only have six full-time program staff, so most of them are members of two or three ministry teams. I serve on the worship team with two other ordained ministers, both of whom are excellent preachers, two part-time specialists, and five lay volunteers. Every Tuesday morning we have a seventy-five-minute meeting of the leaders of the twelve ministry teams plus me, my administrative assistant, and our full-time receptionist."

"Why in the world is the receptionist invited?" challenged one of the five people at that end of the table who were now sharing in this conversation.

"Her job is not simply to greet visitors and answer the telephone. Our goal is that she will be able to respond fully to at least half of all questions, whether they come in person, by voice mail, or over the telephone. She was an active volunteer for over twenty years when her husband died suddenly. She needed a job, and we hired her. She still gives 15 to 20 hours a week as a volunteer as well as a 35- to 40-hour workweek. She knows more about what is going on in our church than anyone else in the world. She saves our paid staff a lot of time by answering questions before they reach the staff. When someone telephones or comes in and she says, 'How may I help you?' the listener receives a message that this lady is both eager and able to help. Therefore that weekly staff meeting becomes one of her sources of information. She knows more about all aspects of our church than any other person on this planet!"

"If I heard you correctly, in thirty years you served five congregations, and each time you moved, you saw a need to change your leadership style," reflected the minister who had initiated what had evolved into a long interrogation of Don Johnson. "Is that correct?"

"Yes, yes, no, and yes," replied Don. "Yes, I have just completed thirty years in the parish ministry, but all thirty years have been with the same congregation. What some people call chapters, I call pastorates. During these thirty years this congregation has evolved from what many identified as a dying rural church into a healthy and comfortable middle-sized exurban parish. The combination of the relocation and the expansion of our weekday ministries made possible by that relocation has enabled us to become a suburban megachurch. Our current meeting place is less than two miles from the site that was the home of this congregation for more than 150 years, but it is a radically different economic, social, and residential environment than it was when this was all farmland. One of our fifth-generation members told me recently that we are now in the sixth chapter of our 153-year history and that while the first chapter covered 123 years, the second chapter began with my coming, and the last five chapters covered only thirty years.

"My wife and I have been married for thirty-two years," continued Pastor Johnson, "and we have been living in the same house for the past twenty-five, but our marriage consists of several chapters. The first was as newlyweds in school. The second was as parents of four young and highly dependent children. A third was as parents of increasingly independent teenagers. The fourth was as empty nesters when our youngest left for college, and the fifth began four years ago when my wife went back into the paid labor force. We did not change our place of residence during these past twenty-five years, but we did move into new roles.

"Yes, I did recognize that when that congregation moved into a new stage or chapter of its history, it did require me to accept new leadership responsibilities.

"No, it was not simply on leadership style. The crucial change was in my role. The biggest contrast is between that first chapter and today. During my first few years, my primary and my only constituency consisted of the members and prospective future members. Today, as I explained earlier, about half the time my primary constituency is our program staff. That includes a hundred volunteers, each of whom gives an average of more than eight hours a week as a member of a program staff team. That does not include most of our teachers, youth counselors, ushers, greeters, and others who contribute huge quantities of time and energy. Their primary relationship to staff is not to me, but to a program staff team. In other words, our program staff teams together constitute a congregation of nearly 200 people. They, plus our lay elders, constitute what some would call my inner circle.

"My role as a leader with them reflects the fact that I am working with highly skilled, knowledge people. That parallels the role of the conductor of a symphony orchestra more than it does the role of the coach of a football team. The leadership style I bring to that role is a reflection of my personality, my generation, my seniority, my gifts, my experience, my theology of the church, my failures, my dreams for the future, and my responsibilities in worship and preaching.

"Yes, you are correct that I saw the need to change my leadership role. No one forced me to change. The easiest course of action would have been to relax and to focus on the role as a shepherd of a congregation averaging 125 to 140 at worship. At that point in the evolution of this congregation, that choice probably would have received the wholehearted support of at least four out of five of the members, and we would still be meeting in that old building with the new addition on that two-acre site. Instead of being surrounded by cornfields, however, we would now be surrounded by single-family homes and clusters of town houses and several new churches. If we had not responded to the need for a full-service, seven-day-a-week church, some other congregation would have come along and filled that void."

"My impression is that it took about twenty-three years for your congregation to grow from an average worship attendance of 50 to over 700, but only about seven years to go from 700 to over 1,500. What has turned out to be the most influential factor that has enabled you to double in seven years?" questioned another listener. "Has it been the larger site, the new building, the increase in the population, your leadership, or simply the momentum you have built up?"

"We pass over anyone who is not optimistic about the future, both theirs and ours."

"That's an easy question," replied Don Johnson with a smile. "It clearly has not been the arrival of thousands of new residents. The three largest Protestant churches in the community in 1970 have all shrunk in size. For us, the answer consists of two parts. The more important of the two is our program staff. We have been able to bring together a group of deeply committed, creative, wise, competent, and enthusiastic people with specialized skills.

"We look for people who are overflowing with a passion for ministry and who are high-energy personalities. Their experience in the secular world has taught them how to be productive workers. We pass over anyone who is not optimistic about the future, both theirs and ours. Every new program staffer is comfortable initiating new ideas and ministries. They all understand the culture of this congregation.

"The second factor is the environment we have created and

nurtured that is supportive of the strengths of highly skilled professional, knowledge workers. My number-one contribution has been to recognize the influence of the work environment and to create and enhance the right environment for staff in a megachurch. My second contribution has been in recruiting competent and creative people who flourish in a supportive environment."

WHAT ARE THE LESSONS?

Perhaps the most important lesson from this conversation with Pastor Don Johnson is the impact of the minister's willingness and capability to change roles. If he had not been able and willing to accept the need to redefine his leadership role, this congregation probably would have plateaued in size long ago.

One alternative is to choose a leadership role appropriate for perpetuating yesterday. Another is to choose a role that will please today's members. A third is to choose a leadership role and style that will enable a congregation to fulfill its potential.

A second and overlapping lesson is the importance of the willingness of the congregation to accept a pastor's conclusion that a new day and a new environment often require a new leadership role for the minister. Pastor Johnson enjoyed the support of a congregation that was open to the appropriate and competent leadership of a visionary and future-oriented pastor. He could have begun his ministry in a highly dysfunctional congregation that would have rejected his leadership. Those churches do exist. While no one knows the number, they may include more than one-half of all Protestant congregations on this continent. Frequently all that is required is the persistent efforts of three to ten volunteer leaders to transform what was a healthy congregation into a dysfunctional church. Don was fortunate that his post-seminary career did not begin in a highly dysfunctional church!

What may be the most subtle lesson is a two-way street. The leadership role of the pastor will be influenced by the institutional environment, and that institutional environment will be influenced, and perhaps transformed, by the leadership of the pastor. Thirty years earlier Don Johnson came to what had been identified as a dying church that wanted a shepherd-preacher. The easy course of action would have been to accept that dual role. Instead, by expanding that to include cheer-leader and evangelist, Don transformed the institutional setting.

This illustrates a fourth lesson, which is the distinction between want and need. The majority of small and middle-sized congregations want a minister to fill the roles of shepherd and preacher. Theological schools tend to prepare students to be scholars and/or shepherds. Many of these congregations need a pastor who is a reassuring cheerleader, a persuasive agent of planned change, a good preacher, and an effective evangelist. That can open the door for the pastor to challenge people with specific, attainable, and measurable goals.

> The work environment of the very large church should be one that is compatible with a premium on excellence.

A fifth lesson is the price of success. When effective leadership in one role changes the congregational environment, that usually means a change in the role of the pastor.[1] Thus when the cheerleader-evangelist role transforms the congregation from one with a low level of self-esteem in which institutional survival dominates the agenda into a comfortable and satisfied parish averaging 125 to 150 at worship, the time may have arrived for the pastor to accept the role as a challenger, or perhaps as a visionary leader.

152

The sixth lesson relates to a central theme of this book: Why do so few Protestant congregations cross what some call "the 800 barrier"? When the need is for more very large congregations, why are there so few?

One answer is the shortage of visionary leaders. Another is the leadership role of the senior pastor and the work environment. What is appropriate for the congregation averaging 500 to 700 at worship rarely is acceptable for the congregation of that size that could and should be doubling or tripling in size. A third part of that explanation is the national shortage of highly skilled, professional, and experienced program specialists. A fourth is a reason that is rarely discussed. This is the work environment. The work environment of the very large church should be one that is compatible with a premium on excellence. The work environment in middle-sized and large congregations usually is compatible with good performance, but rarely demands or encourages excellence.

This distinction requires a senior pastor and at least a few of the volunteer policy makers who (a) understand the culture of a supportive work environment for top-quality knowledge workers,[2] (b) are able and willing to create and nurture that environment required for excellence, and (c) are able and eager to recruit top-quality program staff members. Excellence is the key.

The qualities in the program staff, the leadership role of the senior pastor, and the work environment for that staff that enabled the congregation averaging 500 to 700 at worship to remain on a plateau in size year after year are not what is needed for that congregation to grow into a megachurch. The road that brought that church to this point is not the road to take it into tomorrow.

One of the most subtle lessons was illustrated by what Pastor Johnson admitted was one of his most difficult transitions. For more than thirty years, from childhood through college and seminary, he had been taught that his responsibility was to "do it." That included doing the ministry he was trained and paid to do. Eventually the workload grew to the point that he could not do it all, and he needed help. That changed his responsibility from doing ministry to making sure ministry was done.

The next challenge Don Johnson faced came when that congregation continued to grow and demanded a change in his role. Instead of simply adding more paid staff to make sure ministry was being done, the time had come to create and nurture a work environment that was supportive and protective of top-quality program specialists. Replacing generalists with highly skilled specialists usually also means changing the work environment. That also means a change in the leadership role of the senior pastor. The failure to recognize that often is a major factor in explaining why a congregation plateaus at 400 to 700 in average worship attendance rather than becoming a very large church.

An eighth lesson runs against conventional wisdom. The basic generalization is that the larger the size of the congregation, the lesser the need for broad-based support for innovation and the implementation of new ideas in ministry. The 100-member (member, not average worship attendance) parish needs a large proportion of the members to approve and implement change. In the 700-member congregation, active support from 30 percent usually is sufficient if most of the other 70 percent are indifferent or neutral, but not actually opposed. In the 1,200-member parish, the active support of 3 to 10 percent, coupled with the passive neutrality of the remaining 90 to 97 percent, usually is all of the support required by the visionary leader.

While the magic word was never used, a theme that ran through every one of Pastor Johnson's five "pastorates" was that he accepted and fulfilled a universal demand on every leader who expects to mobilize a following. A leader must be a dealer in hope. Don Johnson accepted and fulfilled that role. He proclaimed a hope-filled vision of tomorrow.

Finally, Don Johnson's account adds a reservation to that frequently heard cliché, "If an increase in the number of very large churches is the goal, long pastorates are a key to achieving that goal."

That is a good, but incomplete, statement. It should include the qualification—a long pastorate by a minister who is able to accept and effectively fulfill a new leadership role when that congregation's future will be determined by the leadership role of the senior pastor.

LEADER OR LEARNED MAN?

The pilgrimage of Pastor Don Johnson also raises another central question: Where do we find the leaders who are able to change their role and adapt their style to a new set of circumstances? One response to that question in recent years has been to focus on theological schools and to demand that they place a greater emphasis on preparing students to be effective leaders. A second response has been to create a growing number of leadership institutes designed to help seminary graduates become more effective leaders.

A useful perspective on this issue has been articulated by Professor Thomas Bender in a discussion of the context and goals of higher education. Bender points out that a central assumption of the American university was the need for the "learned man."

> This concept can be traced back to the Renaissance in Florence, Italy. Subsequently it was brought from western Europe to the United States and became a guiding principle for American higher education.[3]

As theological schools modeled themselves on the university graduate school, a natural and predictable outcome was to design a curriculum that would produce a graduate who could qualify as a learned person. One expression of this would be the pastor who could state the issue in theological terms. A major goal is to produce graduates who are competent in "theological reflection."

For more than three centuries this focus on producing graduates who could qualify as learned persons aroused little dissent. As recently as the 1950s it was not uncommon for the pastor, in terms of years of formal education, to be the best-educated person in the parish and perhaps one of the three or four best-educated persons in the whole community.

The old goal of graduating learned persons was replaced by the demands of the labor force for persons with a high level of competence in a narrowly defined skill.

Then came the 1960s and the escalating demand for specialized expertise. Gradually the great research universities, often driven by the need for financial grants, redefined their mission. The old goal of graduating learned persons was replaced by the demands of the labor force for persons with a high level of competence in a narrowly defined skill. This could be seen in the practice of medicine and the law, in engineering, in finance, in the computer sciences, in physics, in agriculture, and in scores of other disciplines.

As many of these laypersons with a high level of specialized skills became leaders in congregational life and denominational circles, they began to project higher expectations of the clergy in leadership positions. "What is your expert opinion?" "What do you see as the probable consequences of Option A as compared to the probable consequences of Option B?" "As the professional in parish life, what do you recommend we do?" These and similar questions were and are articulated by the laity who have learned to respect expertise. They want more than thoughtful theological reflection. They expect their pastor to be an expert on congregational life.

Three generalizations help to explain why this is a pressing issue in the very large congregation.

1. The larger the size of the congregation, the more complex the life and ministry of that worshiping community.
2. The greater the level of complexity, the more likely the simple and intuitive response will be counterproductive.
3. While the very large congregations account for fewer than 2 percent of all Protestant churches, they do include more than 15 percent of all worshipers, so it is not surprising that they include at least one-fifth of the laity who have been taught by their work environment to seek the advice of highly competent specialists.

Therefore, it is not surprising that in the smaller congregations, where life is relatively simple and a premium is placed on skills in interpersonal relationships, the demand is for a pastor who is a loving shepherd. At the other end of the size spectrum in the very large churches, where congregational life is far more complex and where the volunteers include many highly skilled specialists, the demand often is for a senior minister who is an exceptionally competent and knowledgeable leader.

What is a fair expectation of the theological school that has fewer than a hundred seniors receiving the Master of Divinity degree each year? Should it focus on producing graduates who are skilled in theological reflection? Or graduates who are highly competent in interpersonal relationships and can fill the role of the loving shepherd? Or graduates who go out with a high level of skill in one or two areas of ministry, such as

157

ministries with mature adults or with families with a new baby or never-married young adults or with migrants from the Roman Catholic Church or with adults who are new Christians or with couples in an intercultural marriage or in launching and administering a Christian day school or in non-traditional worship or in transforming the Sunday school into a learning community or in the use of the electronic media or in planting a new mission or in large-group dynamics? Or should that seminary concentrate on equipping graduates who eventually will be the senior pastors of the megachurches of the twenty-first century? Or should the primary focus be on equipping graduates to go out and revitalize congregations with an aging and numerically shrinking membership? Or to specialize in preparing students reared in large metropolitan areas to go out and serve town and country congregations in sparsely populated rural communities?[4]

What is a fair expectation of any one theological school? Nearly everyone agrees that a central criterion in selecting the faculty should be to match the competencies of the professor with the priorities in the mission statement. If the goal is to prepare students to go on to graduate school, then the faculty should include several who have earned a reputation as scholars. If the goal is to turn out loving shepherds, then the faculty should include professors who like people. If the goal is to equip highly skilled ministry specialists, then the faculty must include professors who are specialists in parish ministry.

Or would it be easier to focus on graduating learned persons who excel in theological reflection and return the responsibility for preparing the next generation of parish pastors, program specialists, senior pastors of very large congregations, and loving shepherds to teaching churches and/or denominational agencies and/or parachurch organizations?

Should the primary goal be to graduate learned persons? Or to equip skilled leaders? Is it fair to expect one institution of higher education to do both? Probably not.

158

WHAT DO THE STUDENTS WANT?

This debate on the priorities for theological schools has been influenced by the changing composition of the student body and the expectations they bring with them. This change is illustrated by data on newly ordained ministers in The United Methodist Church.[5]

In 1974, 68 percent of all newly ordained seminary graduates in The United Methodist Church were age thirty and younger. In 1993 that proportion had dropped to 18 percent.

Two-thirds of all newly ordained elders in The United Methodist Church in the 1974–77 era were graduates of theological schools affiliated with that denomination, and one third came from non-UMC schools. For those ordained in the 1990–93 era, fewer than one-half were graduates of UM affiliated seminaries.

The most startling shift, however, was the decline of young male ordinands. In the 1974–77 period, 59 percent of all new UM ordinands were males age thirty and younger. For the 1990–93 classes, that proportion was only 17 percent!

Are these new generations of seminary students looking for a graduate school that will equip them to fill the role of a learned person? Or do they prefer a professional school that will prepare them to serve as transformational leaders? Are those two expectations compatible? Or are they mutually exclusive? Is it reasonable to expect that one theological school could offer a two-track course of study—one designed to equip the learned person and one designed to produce specialists in ministry? What is the urgent need in the parish ministry? For more learned persons? Or for a larger number of transformational leaders?

CHAPTER SIX

Points of Vulnerability

C onventional wisdom suggests that the list of "high-risk" congregations is headed by small churches averaging 25 to 40 at worship. There is considerable truth to that diagnosis, but literally thousands of Protestant churches have been in that size bracket for five to ten or more decades. Most of them have been able to survive because they combine five powerful assets: (1) They represent a meaningful expression of a caring community; (2) they offer continuity with the past; (3) they enjoy a meeting place that has been paid for by previous generations of members; (4) they benefit from a core of committed lay volunteers who love their church; and (5) they have at least one other point of commonality (nationality, occupation, denominational affiliation, kinfolk ties, language, race, doctrinal position, social class, etc.) that reinforces the cohesiveness of that community.

By contrast, Protestant congregations averaging more than 500 at worship tend to be relatively fragile institutions. To be more precise, the congregation averaging more than 500 at worship in 1955 or 1960 was twice as likely to have experienced at least a 50 percent decline in size over the next four decades as did the church that was averaging 25 to 40 at worship in 1955 or 1960.

Medical scientists agree that the most productive response to cancer is early detection. Likewise, the best response to the fragile nature of very large churches is to identify potential problems before they undermine the health and vitality of that worshiping community. Seven signs of future vulnerability surface repeatedly, with the first two tied for the position of most threatening.

ACT YOUR SIZE!

A common temptation for both the paid staff and the volunteer policy makers in the congregation averaging 1,500 at worship is to conceptualize it as similar to the church averaging 500 at worship—only this one serves three times as many people. This is especially common among many of the volunteer leaders and/or paid staff who came from smaller congregations.

The result is a self-fulfilling cycle. By acting the way a large church rather than a very large church or a megachurch should act, the numbers shrink, and within a decade or two, the size is consistent with the revised culture.

Ten examples will illustrate this pattern of counterproductive institutional behavior:

By acting the way a large church rather than a very large church or a megachurch should act, the numbers shrink, and within a decade or two, the size is consistent with the revised culture.

1. What proportion of the members should approve a proposed new ministry before an effort is launched to implement that proposal?

In the small congregation, the ideal answer is 100 percent. The second best is, Everyone either approves or does not articulate dissent. In the congregation averaging 450 to 700 at worship, the typical goal is "broad-based support," or at least 80 percent. In the megachurch the answer is, The majority of the leadership, plus the volunteers required to implement it. Thus in the 3,000-member megachurch, a proposal required $200,000 to implement plus twenty volunteers may be able to mobilize that support from 2 or 3 percent of the membership.

2. In the typical congregation averaging 450 to 700, the governing board often places a high priority on allocating scarce resources (staff time, money, creativity, volunteers, energy) among competing demands. That rationing role places a ceiling on what can be done.

In the best of the megachurches the governing board operates from an abundance, rather than from a scarcity model. It works with the program staff in expanding ministry and challenges the people to provide the resources required to implement creativity.

3. In well over 95 percent of all American Protestant congregations, the driving force in assigning volunteers is to fill vacant slots. In the other 3 or 4 or 5 percent the number-one criterion is, "Will accepting this volunteer role enhance the spiritual and personal growth of this individual?"

4. Most senior ministers are expected to serve as the number-one preacher, the program or ministry director, and the chief administrator. In effect, these are three part-time jobs. Frequently the pastor prefers to accept and fill all three roles. With but a few exceptions, in the megachurch these are recognized as three full-time responsibilities.

An effective strategy for quickly reducing the size of the megachurch is for the newly arrived senior minister to attempt to assume all three of those responsibilities.

5. What should be done when this adult Sunday school class shrinks in numbers by 50 percent and that one experiences a 75 percent reduction in participants? Likewise, what should be done when that circle in the women's organization drops from 15 to 5 regular participants and another decreases in number from 12 to 4? Or when the junior high choir consists of 3 boys and 9 girls, while the number of singers in the senior high choir drops from 30 to 14? The counterproductive strategy is to focus on merging those two adult classes or combining those two circles or incorporating the junior high choir into the senior high choir.

In the best of the megachurches two questions are raised. First, what are we doing or not doing that has produced these declining numbers? Second, what new classes or groups or circles or choirs or organizations or cells or fellowships should we be creating here to meet the needs of those who do not find our existing ministries responsive to their needs?

6. In redesigning the staff configuration the megachurch frequently will replace the departing full-time ordained generalist with three or four or five highly skilled lay specialists.

A widely followed strategy for reducing the size of the megachurch is to replace those highly skilled lay specialists with full-time ordained generalists.

7. The megachurch creates a separate 501(c)3 corporation to serve as a foundation to receive bequests, grants, and special gifts and to encourage deferred giving. The trustees are members who do not currently hold any other policy-making office in that congregation. Income from investments is used for missions and to launch new ministries.

The road to numerical decline calls for placing control of the endowment fund with either the existing board of trustees or the finance committee. Income from investments may be used to balance the operating budget, to meet debt service payments, or to maintain the real estate.

8. Three of the driving forces in the planning in the megachurch are evangelism, an openness to new expressions of ministry, and expanding the group life to be able to accommodate more people.

Three of the driving forces in the decision-making processes in the very large congregation that is shrinking in size are taking better care of today's members, perpetuating local traditions, and maintaining the real estate.

9. The influential yardstick for evaluating new ideas in the numerically growing megachurch is, What is the potential here? In the numerically shrinking congregation, that yardstick is, What is possible here?

10. Back in the 1950s the very large congregation with the eloquent preacher assumed that Sunday morning was when prospective future members made their first contact with that church. In the 1990s that first contact with a megachurch was more likely to come during the week. It might be in a weeknight Bible study group or serving as a volunteer tutor in an after-school program or enrolling a child in a weekday preschool ministry or participation in a recreation program or a Wednesday or Saturday evening worship service or as a volunteer in the church-operated soup kitchen or working on a Habitat For Humanity house or participation in a mutual support group.

The numerically shrinking former megachurch often continues to assume that the initial contact with future members will be on Sunday morning. The numerically growing megachurch recognizes the value of expanding the number and variety of those weekday and weeknight entry points. The "act your size" behavior pattern for the very large churches changed radically between the 1950s and the 1990s in respect to entry points for prospective future members!

WHAT IS THE PLAN OF SUCCESSION?

Why did the congregation that peaked in size with an average worship attendance of over 2,000 shrink to less than half that number in a decade or two?

One answer is that it failed to act like a big church. A frequent overlapping response was that the departure of the visionary leader was followed by a mismatch between the gifts, personality, value system, priorities, skills, and experience of the successor and what that congregation needed at that point in its history. A common example is when the successor came from a successful experience as the senior minister of a much smaller congregation and sought to implant the culture and values of that smaller congregation into the megachurch.

The basic generalization is (a) the larger the size of the congregation and/or (b) the younger the constituency and/or (c) the fewer the number of senior pastors to have served this congregation since 1950 and/or (d) the more central the proclamation of God's Word is in the total ministry of that congregation and/or (e) the greater the degree of diversity among the constituents and/or (f) the smaller the proportion of adults who are closely tied to an adult class and/or (g) the higher the annual rate of turnover among the members, the more likely that the issue of succession in the position of senior minister will become the number-one point of vulnerability in looking at the future of that congregation.

A second basic generalization is (a) the larger the size of the congregation and/or (b) the longer the tenure of the departing senior minister and/or (c) the faster the growth rate and/or (d) the more the design of the ministry is staff-driven (as contrasted with tradition-driven or driven by lay volunteer committees) and/or (e) the larger the proportion of the preaching load carried by the senior minister, the more likely that the culture and continuity reflect the personality of that senior minister.

Those two basic generalizations help to explain why the departure of the long-tenured senior pastor can be highly disruptive.

A third basic distinction reflects the difference between resignation and retirement. The resignation of the senior minister who departs to accept a challenging new opportunity may resemble a divorce. The husband leaves his wife because he is attracted to what sometimes is referred to as a "trophy wife." (Frequently described simply as a "young chick.") Friends and allies may regret his departure, but the period of mourning usually is brief. The chair for the successor may be cold, but at least it is empty.

The retirement of the long-tenured senior pastor frequently resembles a funeral. In the weeks following the memorial service (often called a farewell banquet), several of the pastor's supporters agree, "We didn't do what we should have done while Pat was still here. Let's make up for it by making Pat the Minister of Visitation or by doing what we should have done earlier or by inducting Pat into sainthood." The successor arrives to find that chair is still warm and occupied.

There often is a vast difference between following a saint who continues as a member of that worshiping community and following someone who ran off with a new lover!

The old paradigm called for a national search for a super-star preacher who would come and fill that vacant pulpit. Two trends have undermined that old paradigm in recent years. First, the large congregations have discovered an increasingly severe national shortage of superstar preachers who can serve as a satisfactory successor. Second, the new paradigm places a high premium on secur-ing a good "match" between (a) the person-ality, gifts, priorities in ministry, skills, experi-ence, and place on the theological spectrum of the successor and (b) the culture, priorities, needs, place in the evolution of that worshiping community's journey, role, and public image of the church seeking a new senior minister.

Ideally every very large congregation averaging 800 or more at worship will have prepared a plan of succession.

The highest success rate in recent years in achieving an excellent match has been to choose the successor who has been on the staff for seven to twenty years and thus has been able to (a) understand, affirm, and internalize the unique cul-ture of that large congregation and (b) earn the respect and confidence of the staff and the volunteer leadership.

Ideally every very large congregation averaging 800 or more at worship will have prepared a plan of succession. That plan should include a staff member who could be the heir apparent. The heir apparent should be an effective communicator and preacher, understand and affirm the unique culture of that congregation, and preach on at least forty weekends annually. (This may be on Saturday evening or at one of the Sunday morning services or Monday evening or late Sunday afternoon or evening.)

Too often the decision has been to bring in a successor who concludes, "I've never been in a congregation as large as this one, but with the full cooperation of the staff and the volunteer leaders, I believe we can cut it back to what I'm comfortable with at this point in my career."

WHAT GUIDES THE DECISION-MAKING PROCESSES?

An elder or a task force brings a specific recommendation for consideration. What will be the response of the volunteer leaders and the program staff?

In most congregations the typical response reflects either (a) the respondent's personal opinion and/or (b) the respondent's previous experiences in this or other congregations.

The two relevant basic generalizations are (a) the larger the size of the congregation, the more important it is for major decisions to be made in the larger context of criteria that already have been articulated, discussed, and widely accepted among the leaders, and (b) a high level of intentionality in ministry is an essential central characteristic of the self-identified kingdom-building church. Both generalizations support the assumption that the decision-making process will be consistent with (a) the size of the congregation and/or (b) the self-identified roles.

High on that list of guidelines should be an issue raised elsewhere in this book. Do we conceptualize ourselves as (a) one big extended family or (b) a congregation of classes, cells, circles, fellowships, etc., or (c) a congregation of congregations or (d) a congregation of communities? (See point 9 in chapter 7.)

A dozen other potential guidelines can be cited to illustrate the same basic point.

1. Do we take literally Luke 12:48*b*: "Every one to whom much is given, of him will much be required"? Do we agree that that expectation applies to us, and do we agree that this congregation has been richly blessed by God?

2. Are we convinced that God is calling us to be a kingdom-building congregation or a congregation-building church? Or primarily a maintenance operation?

3. Do we place a high value on optimizing the range of alternatives open to the leaders here ten or fifteen years from now, or are we comfortable limiting the range of choices open to future generations here?

4. The average (mean) size of a Christian congregation in the United States today is approximately triple the (mean) average size in 1900. Do we believe that trend will continue through the twenty-first century? Or do we believe the day of the megachurch is nearing an end and by 2098 the average (mean) size of Christian congregations in America will be a substantially smaller number than today?

5. Do we expect that in the year 2020 this congregation will be about the same size it is today or substantially smaller or substantially larger?

6. Do we believe we can influence that outcome by the way we staff in the year ahead?

7. Do we agree that one of the distinctive assets of our congregation today is, "We know how to do big church exceptionally well"?

8. Do we agree that a central component of a long-term growth strategy is to expand the range of choices we offer in worship, learning, involvement in volunteer ministries, music, and entry points for tomorrow's new constituency?

168

9. Given our present resources, should our number-one priority be on persuading nonbelievers of the truth and relevance of the Christian gospel or on helping believers become better informed and more knowledgeable Christians or on transforming learners into disciples or on equipping parents to transmit the Christian faith to their children or in challenging and equipping disciples to be apostles engaged in doing ministry? (It is rare to find a congregation that can mobilize the resources required to implement more than two of those as the top priority!)

10. In planning for our ministry in the twenty-first century, do we use a three-year time frame? Or five-year? Or seven-year? Or ten-year? Or twenty-year?

11. Should a driving force be to minimize expenditures for program staff?

12. In designing ministry, do we focus primarily on inputs (schedules, expenditures, job descriptions, etc.) or primarily on outcomes? Do we add a second Saturday evening worship service (a) to get better use of our present space or (b) as part of a larger strategy to reach a slice of the population we now are largely missing? Do we add a second preacher to the staff to reduce the workload on our senior minister or to expand the range of choices we offer people?

The absence of an agreed upon set of guidelines can be a major point of vulnerability in the very large congregation. The use of guidelines can minimize the chances that a new and unexpected issue will polarize the congregation.

PARTICIPATION OR PERFORMANCE?

One of the most significant, but largely ignored, differences between small Protestant congregations and the very large churches reflects the values of the constituency. In the typical small congregation a high value is placed on participatory democracy. Every member has a right to be heard. A common goal is that every member will attend and participate in every congregational meeting. In many this is reflected in a constitution that requires a relatively large proportion of the members to be present in order for decisons to be valid. In selecting members of the governing board, an effort often is made to have representation from every faction, class, organization, generation, choir, and group. "Who made that decision?" is a frequently asked question.

By contrast, most of the constituents of the megachurch place a high value on the quality of the decisions. "Was that a good decision?" becomes the criterion, not who made it.

The anonymity and complexity that are characteristics of the megachurch make it difficult for volunteers, who invest only eight to twelve hours a week in the life of that worshiping community, to make informed decisions.

Thus one of the most effective ways to shrink the size of the typical megachurch is to operate with a governing board of thirty or more members reinforced by a rule that every major policy recommendation must be submitted to a congregational meeting at which every member may speak and vote. In several denominations the goal of uniformity includes a rule or a recommendation that every congregation, regardless of size, should utilize the same system of governance. Since the vast majority of congregations average fewer than 150 at worship, that denominational model usually is designed for small churches.

To put it very simply, the structure of a pure democracy in congregational governance and the high level of performance expected by the constituents of the megachurch are incompatible.

SEND MONEY OR DO MISSIONS?

In the 1950s the "tall-steeple churches" frequently were applauded for the amount of money they allocated to missions and sent to their denominational headquarters. The 1960s brought the admonition, "Find your mission in your own backyard and do it." A remarkably large proportion of all churches, and especially the very large congregations, accepted that challenge. Many also discovered that this enhanced their attractiveness to younger generations.

Today most megachurches are engaged in a broad range of missional ministries that do not benefit their own constituents. That list includes planting new missions, sending work crews to missions in other parts of the world, enlisting volunteers for tutoring and mentoring programs, sheltering the homeless, feeding the hungry, visiting those in prison, offering job training opportunities for persons on public assistance, rehabilitating housing, and auto repair services for single-parent mothers.

As they act out their Christian convictions, these congregations become especially attractive to ex-churchgoers who have become disillusioned by the apparent self-centered stance of some churches.

In at least a few religious systems, a high value is still placed on the obligation of individual congregations to collect and send away money to support denominational agencies and programs. The overall trend, however, is for denominational agencies to become financially self-supporting from user fees; contributions from individual donors; grants from foundations, governments, and corporations; income from investments; bequests; and special fund-raising events. That trend is most visible in social-welfare agencies and educational institutions and among parachurch organizations.

If the goal is to reduce the number of megachurches in a particular denominational system, then one component of the strategy is to discourage these congregations from doing missions and to encourage or require them to send more dollars away to hire someone to do ministry on their behalf.

WHAT IS IN THE NEWSLETTER?

What appears on the back page of the Sunday morning bulletin or on the weekly or monthly parish newsletter? The answer is, What the persons in charge of those two channels believe the readers should know.

To be more precise, in the congregation averaging 300 to 700 at worship, those often are filled with (1) the schedule of meetings, rehearsals, events, trips, and classes for the coming week to remind the readers of where they should be and when; (2) invitations for people to attend a special event or service or play or concert; (3) pleas for volunteers to come forward to fill vacancies; (4) a report on that congregation's finances; (5) one or two or three paragraphs of words of gratitude to those who were of help in a special situation; (6) the latest news on those who have been hospitalized; (7) an announcement of the date for the next class of people who want to unite with that congregation; (8) announcements of special training events for volunteers; (9) a column by the pastor or a staff member; and (10) a progress report on the trustees' response to a real estate problem.

In the congregation averaging 2,500 or more at worship, that space is more likely to be filled by (1) the story of one individual's spiritual growth, (2) an inspirational column by the pastor celebrating a victory over adversity by an individual or family, (3) a report on the success of a new ministry launched recently, (4) a letter of thanksgiving from a missionary supported by this congregation, (5) three or four paragraphs introducing a new staff member or describing how a staff member has moved to a new stage of his or her vocational pilgrimage, (6) a report on the effectiveness of a community outreach ministry carried out by this congregation, (7) a brief report on a major congregational victory achieved during the past few weeks, (8) perhaps the names of new members uniting with this congregation during the past week or month,

(9) a eulogy of the life and ministry of a local "saint" or "pillar" who died recently, and (10) a brief account of how this congregation rallied to help a person or family (often anonymous) in distress.

Why the difference?

The first example reflects the hope that every member needs to be fully informed about the basic facts of congregational life and encouraged to be an active participant. The primary audience is that 30 to 60 percent of the resident members who want to know what is going on here every week. The secondary audience is the remaining 40 to 70 percent who should want to be more actively involved.

The second example begins with the assumption that the weekly schedule is too long and too complex to be of interest to everyone. A second assumption is that in a large and anonymous community the people will be encouraged and their loyalty enhanced as they discover what this congregation is doing in ministry. The primary audience consists of first-time visitors and recently arrived new constituents. The goal is to help them learn how this church is making a difference in the lives of individuals and in the larger community. A secondary audience includes those members who welcome some "bragging points" to use as they talk about church with their colleagues at work, neighbors, relatives, friends, and acquaintances.

At this point a few readers may object that this overstates the importance of internal communication.

One reason to emphasize this issue is symbolism. A common pattern is a shift in focus following the arrival of a new senior minister or a new editor of that newsletter. For a decade or more, as that congregation grew into a megachurch, the content resembled the second example described here. As time passed, however, the pressures to become more member-oriented increased. This change (a) paralleled a plateauing or decline in numbers and (b) became highly visible in the content included in the Sunday morning bulletin and/or the parish newsletter.

A second reason to examine this subject is it provides a good test of the level of intentionality in decision making. The most widely used criterion in deciding what should be included in these two channels of communication is precedent—What did we include in previous years? A better system asks four questions:

1. Who is the primary audience? Who is the secondary audience?
2. What are the messages we want to deliver to these two audiences?
3. Are these two channels among the best ways to deliver those messages to those two audiences?
4. How do we deliver the messages that will be excluded from these two channels? (E.g., bulletin boards in corridors may carry the weekly schedule or photographs of recent new members.)

A third reason is to test the system. The basic generalization is that the larger the size of the congregation and/or the faster the growth rate and/or the larger the geographical area served and/or the greater the degree of diversity within the constituency and/or the longer that congregation has been in existence and/or the larger the number of weekly worship services, the greater the need for a high-quality and redundant internal communication system.

A common pattern is for a large church to outgrow its internal communication system, plateau in the number of regular participants as many people feel a loss of the sense of belonging, and eventually decline numerically.

Fourth, a high-quality internal communication system is the best way to combat the disruptive impact of false rumors.

Finally, in today's world this also is a good test of that congregation's capability to utilize modern technology. Computers and desktop publishing make it relatively easy to include late news in that Sunday morning bulletin and to custom design a bulletin for each service. An interesting innovation is the ten- to fifteen-minute videotape produced every week that recaptures in pictures the highlights in

... a high-quality internal communication system is the best way to combat the disruptive impact of false rumors.

the life and ministry of that congregation over the past seven days. One videotape may include the arrival of a baby, two or three weddings, volunteers working on a Habitat For Humanity house, a newly organized adult Bible study group, a work trip by a youth group, a visit to a new mission sponsored by this congregation, volunteers working at a shelter for the homeless, a visit to one part of the weekday children's ministry, a eulogy of a member who died recently, and a thirty-second introduction to next week's sermon.

One way to increase the proportion of worshipers who are seated well before the beginning of a worship service is to project that week-in-review videotape in the period before the beginning of the service. If the schedule does not permit that, the videotape is shown on monitors in the corridors or narthex.

The Internet now makes it possible to have an interactive web site that provides news of the congregation that is updated several times daily as constituents add or amend messages.

THE DISPLACEMENT SYNDROME

"My wife and I joined this congregation twenty-eight years ago," recalled a sixty-four-year-old member in a conversation with his thirty-nine-year-old pastor at the West Hills Church. "At that time, this was an eleven-year-old new mission, and we averaged about 125 at worship. One reason why we came here was we didn't want to be part of a small church where we would be overloaded with requests to serve as volunteers for this or that. We also didn't want the anonymity and complexity that are characteristics of the big churches. We were looking for a middle-sized congregation, and we found it here. For our first twenty-plus years, we were happy. This continued to be a great example of a solid middle-sized church. According to the annual reports, with two exceptions, every year our average church attendance ranged between 120 and 140. When the Reverend Burke retired, we were afraid the good times might come to an end, but from day one of your arrival, we were impressed with your leadership, your energy, and your emphasis on reaching unchurched people. After all, that's what it's all about."

"What's the point you're trying to make?" interrupted the pastor, who had watched this man change in eight years from being one of the pillars at West Hills to a person who never missed his adult Sunday school class and who rarely was absent from Sunday morning worship, but who now did not participate in any other facets of the ministries and programs.

"The reason I made an appointment to come to see you this morning was to explain why my wife and I are leaving West Hills Church. This is not the church we joined twenty-eight years ago. According to the annual report for last year, the average worship attendance was 817. This is growing into what some people call a megachurch. It is way beyond what we used to describe as a big church. We've been talking about this for several months, and last Sunday on the way home from church we decided the time had come to leave."

"Why did you come to that conclusion?" asked the pastor. "What are the reasons for you two to leave after being here for most of your married life?"

"Well, I've already told you one reason. We feel more comfortable in a middle-sized church where everyone knows everyone else. You came and changed all of that. When you added a second service to the Sunday morning schedule, you changed all of that. We're now two congregations, the early service crowd and the late service crowd. We felt the old schedule of Sunday school followed by worship was the best way to reinforce the ties of the people to one another. You're more interested in numbers than in relationships.

"Second, you've brought in hundreds of new members in your time here. Some came and left after a year or two or three, but many are still here. In order to attract them, you changed the ministry of music. We used to have an organist, and we sang the classic hymns of the Christian faith. Now you have a praise band at the early service and an orchestra at the second. I don't know what you do on Saturday evening, but we miss the old music tradition here.

"Third, you have encouraged the nominating committee to choose the new leaders and officers from among the people who joined since you came. A lot of us who were the pillars here for decades have been replaced by strangers, none of whom ever come to us to ask our advice. A lot of us old-timers feel that when we come here now, we are visiting somebody else's church. Some of our friends, who also are longtime members here, were over to our house for dinner a few weeks ago, and I was intrigued when the conversation got around to what's going on here in this church. Every pronoun was in the third person. Our friends talked about 'they' and 'them.' No one ever used pronouns like 'we' or 'our.'

"Since you asked," continued this unhappy ex-pillar, "another reason we're leaving is we've become convinced we're not needed here. I retired two years ago, and my wife will retire from her job next month. We want to be in a church where we're needed. We now will be able to contribute fifteen to twenty hours a week to the ministries of the church. You have more volunteers and potential volunteers here than you can ever use, and you've made it clear that you prefer to work with people from your generation rather than our generation. Please understand, we're not complaining. We understand why you prefer younger leaders and officers, but if we're not needed, we might as well leave and go to a church that can use some experienced volunteer help. My wife and I are thankful that we're both in good health, so we might as well use the remaining years God has given us to serve where we're needed.

"Finally, as you are well aware, a lot of our friends who were here when you came are no longer around. A half dozen have died. A few have retired to the Sunbelt, others moved to be closer to their children, and at least four couples have left for other churches. The Sunday school class my wife and I helped organize twenty-four years ago ran around 25 to 30 in attendance for years. We're now down to about 15. No one on the staff seems interested in suggesting our class as an attractive option to the new members. It is nearly two years since we had anyone new come to our class, and they came because the wife's sister is a longtime member of our class. It is one thing for a class to die of old age. It's an entirely different issue when an adult Sunday school class dies of neglect! My wife and I decided we would be happier in a church where we can meet and make some new friends."

What's happening here?

The most obvious issue came with the retirement of the sixty-year-old Reverend Burke after a twenty-year pastorate at West Hills Church. His successor was thirty-one when he arrived. Whenever the age of "our pastor" suddenly drops by twenty or more years, that change usually is accompanied by a variety of reactions. Those members who perceived themselves "to be young compared to our pastor" suddenly are old. The young fifty-three-year-old lay leader becomes an old fifty-four-year-old.

Most of us naturally tend to build our social network with

people of our generation. The most highly visible example of this is the birthday party for a three-year-old child. Close behind is that group of young never-married adults, ages nineteen to twenty-five, who "hang out" together. A third example is the group of retired men who have lunch at the church every Tuesday. A fourth example is the new pastor who finds it relatively easy to build ties with members from the same generation, but tends to focus on the role of the shepherd when relating to parishioners who are a couple of decades older. To go from being "one of our pastor's three or four closest personal friends" to being one of several score (or hundred) parishioners is a **big** demotion!

Overlapping that is another dynamic. In only a few years this mature leader went from being a key pillar to "one of our older members." He felt he was being displaced. The primary reason he felt that way was that he was displaced. He felt he was being reclassified from essential to expendable. The reason why he felt that way was because he now was widely perceived by the new leadership as unessential. This feeling was reinforced by his retirement from the labor force. That big retirement dinner usually is designed to ease the pain of being reclassified from essential to expendable. At West Hills Church that feeling was reinforced by the Education Committee's request, "Your Sunday school class no longer needs a room this large. Would you folks be willing to move to a smaller room so we can use this room for a new class we're organizing?" The message received was, "We have a cemetery plot for this class on the third floor, and we want to use this room for a new class of people who are essential to the future of our church."

The pastor at West Hills Church was surprised and distressed by this conversation, which also increased his load of guilt for that week. What made it an even more difficult day began two hours earlier when the director of Christian Education came in to deliver an ultimatum.

179

"I've been thinking about the goal you announced two months ago that, now that we have acquired the eleven-acre parcel of land next door, we should be able to double in size during the next ten years. I want you to know I support that goal, but I need help, and I need it right now if you expect me to double our educational ministry! I'm already overworked. When I came on staff five years ago, I came into a full-time job with nearly 300 children, youth, and adults involved in our educational program. We've added a big program for Wednesday evening for all ages, nearly tripled the size of our children's Sunday school, and started six new adult Bible study groups that meet weekly at some time other than Sunday morning. I think that's pretty good in only five years! The only additional help I've been given is a half-time secretary. If you expect me to double the size of our present program in ten years, I need at least one full-time specialist in children's ministries plus a part-time person to work with the adults, and we need to go from a part-time to a full-time secretary. I was comfortable with the size and nature of this job when I came on staff, but now I feel overwhelmed by the demands on my time and energy. Instead of trying to double the size of this congregation in ten years, why don't we challenge 400 or 500 of our members to go out and be the nucleus for a new mission that would be a big church from day one?"

"First of all, I'm afraid I did not speak very clearly when I challenged our people, and our staff, to double in a decade," began the pastor. "What I meant to communicate was that the time has come to reconceptualize our ministry and act like a church that averages 1,500 to 1,800 at worship. That will require many changes, including changes in my role here and also in your responsibilities. The goal I tried to articulate was a redefinition of the identity, role, and self-image of this congregation. I thought I made it clear that doubling in size should not be seen as a goal but rather as a consequence of our redefinition of what God is calling us to be and to be doing at

West Hills. That was the argument we used to secure permission to raise the money to buy that eleven-acre parcel next door. I recognize some people thought we were buying it simply to secure more parking, but a larger dream drove that decision."

"Okay, I guess I'm one of those who thought you were projecting a goal of doubling in size," commented this staff member. "Now you're telling me you want to redefine my role. Please tell me what that means."

"We talked about that at our quarterly staff retreat a little over three months ago," replied the pastor with a slight degree of impatience. "At that time I explained that I thought the time had come to switch from a producer-oriented emphasis on teaching to a consumer-driven focus on learning. I explained that instead of concentrating on what our people should learn, we should place a greater emphasis on designing ministries in response to what our people felt they needed to learn."

"In other words, you want to put the inmates, rather than the trained professionals like me, in charge of the asylum?"

"I remember you made that same comment at that all-day staff retreat," recalled the pastor. "I will give you the same answer I gave you that day. My dream is to transform this congregation into a big learning community of smaller learning communities. In some of these, the focus will be on what we, the staff here, believe people need to learn. In most of these smaller learning communities, however, the primary focus will be on what the Christian faith offers in response to their self-identified needs, hopes, dreams, fears, problems, hurts, concerns, and questions."

"Maybe what we should do is to divide my job into two. I'll continue as your director of Christian Education and take responsibility for designing and staffing with the right volunteers the educational program that concentrates on what our people need to learn. That's what I thought the job called for

181

when I came on board five years ago, and I believe I have done a pretty good job of doing that. You can find someone else to come in and be director of the Learning Community. To tell you the truth, I'm not at all sure I even understand what that means, much less what accepting responsibility for doing it means."

What's happening here?

The most obvious issue is the lack of adequate communication between this senior pastor and this staff member. This pastor apparently had assumed that if the program staff members heard him articulate his dream, that meant (a) in a few hours they could and would fully comprehend what he had devoted scores of hours to formulating, and (b) after hearing the dream articulated, they would not only completely understand it, but also fully support the implementation of it.

A second issue is it appears that the West Hills Church has outgrown the director of Christian Education. The old role and responsibilities have been replaced by a new role. The old role called for the director of Christian Education, with the help of dozens of volunteer teachers, to do Christian education. That job has grown to be too large for one person. The time has come, however, to abandon that approach and replace it with one in which program staff focus on making ministry happen, not on unilaterally doing it.

A third is staffing. Five years ago the design called for hiring paid professionals to do ministry. When that load grew to more than one person could carry, a common solution was to divide the load and hire more paid staff. One would be responsible for the children's educational program, another for youth ministries, a third for young adults, and so forth.

"As I explained to you and the rest of the staff at our retreat three months ago," continued the senior minister, "we also are changing the way we staff. As you know, we're in the process of creating a worship team that includes four volunteers, me, and two part-time staffers to design worship here as we move into the electronic era. We also are beginning to build a team of fifteen people, eleven of whom are volunteers, plus our parish nurse and three other part-time people, to staff our ministry of pastoral care. Likewise, we want to create a team of one full-time, perhaps three part-time, plus a dozen volunteers to staff the ministry of learning. We may not be ready to do that for at least another six months, but that is a part of the larger design to shift from a staff of full-time professionals to a staff of teams. One of the questions we will have to talk about is whether or not you want to make that change."

This senior minister apparently has concluded that the time has come for at least two paradigm shifts. One is to replace that traditional emphasis on teaching with a new emphasis on learning. The second is to introduce a radically different design for staffing the ministries at the West Hills Church.

One result is that this director of Christian Education feels threatened. A second result is

Displacement usually produces feelings of alienation.

that this hardworking staff member is beginning to feel displaced. One reason for these feelings is that the continuity with the past is being threatened. Another is that this staff member's area of expertise is being challenged. A third reason is that the proposed role as a member of a team is radically different from the old role of being head of my own empire.

The point of both illustrations is the frequent misdiagnosis of what is happening. It would be easy to dismiss the discontent of that long-tenured pillar as resistance to change. It also would be easy to diagnose the objections of this director of Christian Education to what had been proposed and discussed in great detail at that quarterly staff retreat as a desire to protect one's own empire. In both cases, the real issue is displacement. Both of these individuals feel that the comfortable environment they formerly enjoyed at the West Hills Church has been undermined by this senior minister.

Displacement usually produces feelings of alienation. A normal, natural, and predictable consequence of displacement is to seek to identify the person responsible. Frequently that scapegoat is the senior minister. Frequently at least one or two staff members plus several long-tenured volunteer pillars and ex-pillars agree on that diagnosis.

One alternative is to accept the departure of these displaced persons as a normal, natural, and unavoidable consequence of radical change. A second alternative is to invest the extra effort required to help these displaced persons find, accept, and fill a new role. A third alternative is to slow the pace of change and minimize the number of changes made in any one year as part of a larger strategy to reduce the feelings of displacement. (One example is that instead of relocating to a new site, the congregation becomes a two-site church.) A fourth alternative is to focus, not on the departure of these displaced saints, but rather on enlisting a new generation of volunteers and of new paid staff members.

Most important of all, however, is to recognize that the displacement syndrome is a common point of vulnerability as the large congregation grows into the ranks of today's megachurches.

CHAPTER SEVEN

Reservations and Questions

Many years ago a journalist described the Ford Foundation as a large body of money surrounded by people who want to get their hands on that money. The contemporary megachurch often can be described as a large worshiping community surrounded by a ring of tourists seeking to experience it and a larger ring of critics who enjoy articulating reservations and questions about the relevance and viability of those very large congregations. These critics, and some of the tourists, however, do raise questions that deserve serious consideration.

IS IT A PERSONALITY CULT?

One of the most frequently heard criticisms is that the megachurch is a heretical cult that places the charismatic personality of the preacher, rather than Jesus Christ, at the focal point of congregational life. While that generalization may have relevance to a few very large congregations, as well as to thousands of smaller churches with a beloved pastor who arrived thirty years ago, it reflects an overly simplistic assumption about a highly complex institutional issue. A better way to state the question would be to ask what is the central organizing principle that can be used to transform a larger and relatively heterogeneous collection of unrelated individuals into a closely knit and unified community.

The easiest answer to implement is to identify a common enemy and organize the people against that enemy. Adolf Hitler used that organizing principle in Germany in the 1930s. It was a highly effective organizing principle in the post-December 7, 1941, era in the United States. It is widely used by organized labor and by community organizers.[1] Whether that organizing principle can be used by Christians is questionable. Jesus taught that we should love our enemies.

An alternative is to organize the people around the personality of the magnetic, highly visible, long-tenured, and exceptionally articulate leader.

A third is to organize in support of common goals. A fourth is to organize around a precisely stated ideological position. A fifth is to focus on perpetuating local traditions. A sixth is to rally people in support of the maintenance of a sacred meeting place. A seventh is to advance an attractive cause such as missions or evangelism. An eighth is to identify an unmet need shared by many people and to organize to meet that need. A ninth is to build on the positive threads in the history of that organization and to enlist people to help perpetuate that history. A tenth is to focus on the common characteristics of a constituency (nationality, race, social class, language, place of birth, marital status, gender, age, vocation, education, religious affiliation, etc.) and to use that as a central organizing principle. An eleventh is to invite those discontented with the status quo to come together to help pioneer the new. A twelfth is to create a local organization as part of the support system for a larger organization such as a political party or a service club or a denomination or a lodge or a reform movement.

The easiest and quickest way to plant a new mission that averages at least three hundred at worship by the end of the first month is to combine three or four compatible organizing principles. These could include (1) relevant and high-quality biblical teaching and preaching designed to speak to the religious needs of adults on a self-identified faith pilgrimage; (2) ministries designed to help parents rear their children and to transmit the Christian faith to younger generations; (3) the lure of helping to pioneer the new; (4) a clearly and precisely stated missional thrust beyond the immediate constituency; and (5) a clearly stated belief sytem. It helps if this effort is initiated by adults headed by a highly skilled leader who is a charismatic personality and who also recognizes the value of humor. That does describe the early years of several contemporary megachurches, but the personality of that magnetic leader is only one of several central organizing principles. It may be the most highly visible factor to outsiders, but ideally it is only one of several variables.

As the years roll by, as that original magnetic personality is replaced by a successor, and as what began as a movement evolves into a structured organization with rules, precedents, duly elected leaders, local traditions, and a distinctive community image, the need is for continued reliance on a series of redundant or mutually reinforcing organizing principles.

One alternative is to seek another magnetic personality as the successor. An attractive alternative is to seek a successor who can (a) translate wishes, dreams, visions, hopes, and potentialities into an internally coherent, consistent, and operational agenda and (b) create the alliances required to implement that challenging agenda.

BUT WHERE ARE THE POOR PEOPLE?

One of the most common criticisms of the contemporary very large congregations is the absence of the very poor. With a couple of reservations, that reflects a description of reality. One reservation is that while the very poor may not be among the members, they often work there. Many very large congregations have undertaken an intentional, systematic, and constructive effort to create entry-level jobs for the very poor. They work as custodians, in the kitchen, as security staff, and as helpers in the weekday children's ministries, where they can learn the skills and work habits required for them to secure employment in the private sector.

187

If one divides the American adult population into tenths based on income, education, employment and social status, the top tenth, and especially the liberal elite, are underrepresented in the very large Protestant churches.

Likewise, the bottom 20 percent also are underrepresented. Why?

In an exceptionally insightful book, Richard Dunagin suggests four explanations for the absence of the very poor. Citing the research of Charles Lee Williamson, Dunagin points out that if the American population is divided into nine socioeconomic categories, very few people socialize across more than three levels.[2] This means that if a congregation draws most of its constituents from the second, third, and fourth highest levels, it will be extremely difficult to attract people from the lowest two or three levels.

Second, poor people tend not to be joiners, and big institutions draw largely from among people who are joiners. Joiners have practiced the art of becoming part of a large organization.

Banfield argued that the critical line of demarcation separating the lower class from the upper class is the time horizon of the individual.

Third, the experiences of many poor people have taught them that large organizations cannot be trusted. They tend to perceive large organizations as anonymous, complex, and impersonal forces that exploit the poor.

Fourth, poor people seek intimacy and simplicity. As was emphasized earlier, megachurches tend to be marked by anonymity and complexity. The poor often play out of a rule book different from the one followed by the middle class.

Thirty years ago Edward C. Banfield published a pair of books in which he suggested that the most relevant indicator of social class is not education, income, employment, or housing. Banfield argued that the critical line of demarcation separating the lower class from the upper class is the time horizon of the individual. The upper class are characterized by a long time frame; they are willing to sacrifice immediate gratification for future rewards. The lower class think and act in terms of today. They choose immediate gratification over future satisfaction.[3]

Banfield's thesis does greatly oversimplify an exceptionally complex subject, and it evoked a huge negative response; but it does help to explain why most megachurches do not reach the poor. The typical megachurch teaches and advocates deferred gratification, while lower-class people live in a world that places a premium on immediate satisfaction.

Eight Exceptions

While it is true that most urban and suburban megachurches do not reach and serve people from the very top or the bottom of the socioeconomic pyramid, there are many exceptions.

The least publicized may be those megachurches that do draw large numbers of upper-class constituents. Their common characteristic is the proclamation of a clearly and precisely stated belief system that displays a high degree of internal consistency and coherence and that is preached and taught with absolute certainty and zero ambiguity.

A second and rapidly growing exception is the predominantly Anglo megachurch with a constituency drawn largely from the upper half of the socioeconomic ladder that reaches and serves poor people, ethnic minority groups, and younger generations through a network of off-campus ministries. These off-campus ministries usually are initially staffed by volunteers from that missionary church, but eventually are staffed with indigenous leaders.[4]

A third exception is the charismatic, or "Spirit-filled," megachurch that promises hope to the hopeless.

A fourth exception is the megachurch in which the number-one central organizing principle is the dream of a better life for one's children. These churches attract the poor who are driven by powerful, upwardly mobile ambitions for their children. Frequently one institutional expression of this is the Christian day school.

A fifth exception consists of those megachurches that preach a "prosperity gospel" that also legitimates the priority given to immediate satisfaction.

While relatively few in number, several dozen megachurches that include the poor are organized around the principle that the charter members shared a common birthplace (a rural southern community, Southeast Asia, etc.), they migrated to a strange place for political or economic reasons that did not welcome them, and church became that highly valued "third place" in their new life.

A seventh exception is the very large African American congregation that places a premium on active and highly visible roles for black men.

An eighth exception is the megachurch that is organized around the magnetic personality of a preacher who is able to articulate, legitimate, and affirm the hopes and fears of the poor and the hopeless. Their critics often refer to these preachers as demagogues.

Whether the megachurches of 2030 will draw most of their constituents from the broad middle of the socioeconomic pyramid or from among the poor is a question yet to be answered.

WHO WILL CREATE THE NEXT GENERATION OF CHRISTIAN INSTITUTIONS?

The nineteenth century brought the creation of huge numbers of Christian colleges, mission societies, theological schools, hospitals, orphanages, and other institutions. Many trace their origins to the initiative of one congregation, but eventually were adopted by a denominational system. The 1865–1975 era saw many new Christian institutions created, financed, and administered by denominations. That list includes camps, housing for low-income households, colleges, hospitals, retreat centers, seminaries, social-welfare agencies, retirement villages, and nursing homes.

Many of these have become administratively independent and are financially self-supporting. Others rely on annual financial subsidies from denominational sources. One argument is that a financial subsidy is necessary to maintain the tie to the denomination. A counterargument is that scarce denominational resources should be directed to giving birth to the new rather than subsidizing the old.

The second half of the 1990s saw the United States Congress, corporations, foundations, local governments, and individuals giving more support for the creation of new social-welfare efforts by faith communities. One result is the creation of thousands of single-purpose 501(c)3 nonprofit corporations by individual congregations. Several have received multimillion-dollar grants from the federal government. Will denominational agencies create a new generation of Christian institutions for the third millennium? Or will that responsibility for new responses to new needs be met largely by the megachurches? Time will tell.[5]

HOW MUCH LAND?

The biggest unknown in predicting the future of the megachurch may be decided by the United States Supreme Court early in the twenty-first century.

All across the country congregations are meeting rejection by local officials when they propose to buy a parcel of land for a meeting place. One official objects that the proposed use of the

191

land does not meet the standard of the "highest and best use." Others object to removing that property from the tax roll. Neighbors object to the potential increase in traffic. In many municipalities a church is defined as a special use and must receive specific approval before a building permit can be granted.

One reason for these objections is the need for more land. In the 1950s a three-acre church site was perceived as somewhere between adequate and extravagant. Today the congregation averaging 4,000 at worship that includes a Christian day school through grade eight, a retirement village, a weekday child-care ministry, a retreat center, a seminary extension, a large-scale outdoor recreation program, ten acres of off-street parking, seven-day-a-week programming, and adequate open space for setbacks and storm water control needs 90 to 120 acres. Is that too much land to be removed from the tax roll? Or would it be easier for municipal officials to approve a dozen five-acre church sites, a completely separate eight-acre site for an elementary school, a twenty-acre site for a modest retirement complex, a five-acre retreat center, and a ten-acre neighborhood park, playground, and swimming pool?

Currently many congregations have been advised that they have two choices. One is to modify and reduce their plans in order to secure municipal approval. The alternative is to be prepared to invest up to three years and a million dollars in litigation in which they probably would prevail eventually—but can they afford that much time and money?

The question of who will create the new generation of Christian institutions may be decided on the basis of land-use decisions by the courts.

WHAT IS THE FUTURE OF
OFF-CAMPUS MINISTRIES?

Should we relocate to a larger parcel of land and construct new facilities, or should we remain at this sacred place and invest our money in purchasing small parcels of land here for additional parking and in renovating these old buildings?

A growing number of congregations are answering that either/or question with a "Yes" response. This strategy calls for the addition of a second meeting place, usually three to ten miles away, but calls for continuing as one congregation with one governing board, one budget, one treasury, one staff, and one identity.

This two-site model may have 1,000 worshipers every week at one site and 500 to 2,500 at the other location. This two-site model also is being substituted for the old strategy that large congregations should "mother" or plant new missions.

Another expression of the off-campus model is motivated by a desire to reach people who would never enter that impressive and intimidating building housing that upper-middle-class Anglo congregation. One off-campus site is chosen to reach young adults in the 18-24 age bracket, a second to reach a group of recent immigrants from the Pacific Rim, a third to reach single-parent mothers in low-income housing, a fourth to reach a Latino group, a fifth to serve residents of a mobile home court, a sixth to serve a group of mothers whose husbands are in jail or prison, and a seventh to serve residents of a public housing complex. Thus one congregation may have 1,000 or more people worshiping at the "home campus" every weekend plus 100 to 2,000 worshiping at the 3 to 200 off-campus sites every weekend.

... the most difficult strategy to implement, would be the revitalization of tradition-driven and numerically shrinking congregations organized before 1950 that now are serving an aging constituency.

The unknown is whether this trend is (1) a creative response to the cost of land or (2) a passing phenomenon or (3) an exceptionally effective evangelistic strategy or (4) the easiest way to create a multicultural congregation or (5) a promising new way to define the word *congregation*.

WHAT IF IT DOES HAPPEN?

A central thesis of this book is that the number of Protestant congregations in the United States now averaging a thousand or more at worship could and should at least double during the next two or three decades. This would be a central component, along with planting at least a couple of thousand new missions annually, of a larger strategy to reach new generations of American-born residents and recent immigrants with the gospel of Jesus Christ. A third component of this larger strategy could be the creation of new expressions of worshiping communities. A fourth, and by far the most difficult strategy to implement, would be the revitalization of tradition-driven and numerically shrinking congregations organized before 1950 that now are serving an aging constituency.

Every major change produces unanticipated consequences. What would be some of the consequences if the number of megachurches doubled between 2000 and 2020?

Which Career Path?

The Crossroads Church was founded in 1986, and by 1992 it was averaging 575 at weekly worship. The next few years turned that sharp growth curve into a plateau. In response to deteriorating health, the founding pastor chose early retirement in 1998. Before beginning the search for a successor, the volunteer leaders decided to design an aggressive evangelistic strategy that called for doubling worship attendance in seven years. Where will they look to enlist the staff to help implement that strategy?

The old conventional wisdom called for challenging a young pastor serving a congregation averaging 300 to 500 at worship to become the new senior pastor. Recent history suggests a more productive approach may be to invite the senior associate minister of a congregation averaging 1,000 to 1,500 at worship to become the successor to that departed founding pastor. The explanation is to look for a minister who brings firsthand and contemporary experience on the staff of a very large congregation rather than someone who brings small or middle-sized church experience.

What does this say to the seminary senior who feels a call to become the senior pastor of a megachurch? Should that career path from seminary begin with serving one or two small congregations, followed by serving a middle-sized church, followed by leading a large congregation, followed by eventual promotion to a megachurch? Or should that seminary senior begin by planting a new mission designed to grow into a megachurch? Or would a more logical career path begin by going from seminary to a program staff position with a megachurch, followed by becoming one of the two regular preachers in another megachurch, followed by a "demotion" to become the senior minister of a large congregation ready to grow into a megachurch?

A Loss of Jobs?

Perhaps the most highly visible consequence of an increase in the number of very large churches would be a decrease in the number of jobs in the parish ministry for seminary-trained, full-time, fully credentialed and ordained ministers. This can be illustrated by comparing two scenarios. One is a megachurch averaging 3,800 at worship. Their paid program staff includes seven full-time and fully credentialed ordained ministers, two part-time seminary graduates, both of whom hold full-time secular jobs, plus six full-time lay program specialists and thirty part-time lay program specialists. Their payroll also includes two semiretired pastors who are compensated on the basis of quarter-time work.

The regional judicatory of a mainline denomination overlaps the service area of this megachurch. That regional judicatory includes 70 congregations with a combined weekly worship attendance of 7,200. Those 70 congregations are served by 45 full-time seminary graduates (4 senior ministers, 6 associate pastors, 18 other ministers each serving one congregation, 15 who serve two congregations, and 2 who serve a three-church yoked parish) plus 4 part-time retired ministers and 8 bivocational pastors.

That regional judicatory includes nearly twice as many worshipers every week as the one megachurch, but it provides full-time jobs for forty-five seminary-trained ministers, six times as many jobs as that megachurch supplies. That comparison overlooks the fact that two of the seven full-time ministers on the staff of the megachurch never attended seminary and three others earned their degrees while serving on the staff of that megachurch and attending classes on a part-time basis at a seminary extension center.

The shortage of attractive pastorates for new seminary graduates is now described as a "problem." By 2030 it could become a crisis.

Senate or House?

A more subtle consequence can be discussed in the context of one of the great compromises in the writing of the Constitution of the United States. What will be the basis for representation? The compromise was that each state would be entitled to two members in the United States Senate, but representation in the House of Representatives would be based on population.

In the regional judicatory described earlier, the largest congregation is entitled to six delegates—three clergy and three lay delegates—who represent the 1,150 members. A 200-member congregation is entitled to two delegates—the pastor plus one layperson. Should that 4,900-member megachurch, if it were a member of that regional judicatory, be entitled to fourteen delegates (seven clergy and seven laity) or forty-nine (one per 100 members—the ratio for that 200-member congregation)?

Is it reasonable to expect that churchgoers who feel that they are seriously underrepresented in denominational decision-making processes will be generous financial supporters of those decisions?

Should the rule book for the new millennium call for the representation of institutions or of people?

Denominational Generalists or Specialists?

One of the consequences already can be seen in the criteria used to select program staff members for denominational agencies. The old debate was between choosing generalists who would work with all types of churches within a relatively small geographically defined area versus choosing specialists who would serve a more narrowly defined agenda but cover a much larger geographical area.

The differences between the smaller one-half of all American Protestant congregations (those reporting an average weekly worship attendance of 75 or fewer) and the larger half have resulted in the emergence of scores of specialists who focus on the distinctive culture, role, and needs of the smaller churches.

The differences in the culture, role, and needs between congregations averaging 1,800 at worship and those averaging 300 or 400 or 500 are equally great. Does this suggest that those denominations that are encouraging the emergence of more megachurches should have program staff specialists who focus their efforts on the very large churches? If the answer is yes, should those specialists be on the staff of regional judicatories? Or on the national staff? Or is it more realistic to expect program staff of regional judicatories to be equipped to resource congregations of all sizes and types? Or should the megachurches and potential megachurches turn to parachurch organizations for resourcing?

More Competitive?

At the beginning of the third millennium American Protestantism included approximately 5,000 to 6,000 congregations that reported an average worship attendance of 800 or more. Moving down the size scale, for every congregation averaging 700 to 1,050 at worship, there were six or seven reporting an average worship attendance of 350 to 700. What would be the consequences if one out of six of those churches currently averaging 350 to 700 at weekly worship doubled or tripled or quadrupled in size? One result would be the proportion of all Protestant congregations averaging 800 or more at worship would climb from approximately 1.7 percent to 3 percent. Add in another 2,000 new missions that quickly grew into the megachurch bracket, and that could mean 3.5 percent of the 300,000 Protestant churches in the United States would be averaging 800 or more at worship. (This assumes that none of the existing very large congregations would shrink in numbers and thus drop out of that size bracket. That is unlikely! A more realistic projection calls for 2,000 new megachurches to be created in the first decade or so of the twenty-first century to replace an estimated 2,000 that will shrink out of the very large church category. Who will plant 150 to 200 new missions annually that are designed to become megachurches? Entrepreneurial pastors? Denominational agencies? Existing megachurches? The loosely affiliated religious movements

198

such as the Vineyard? Existing independent churches? The regional judicatories of the mainline Protestant denominations? The new denominations born since 1900?)

A net increase of even 4,000 or 5,000 in the number of congregations averaging more than 800 at worship would increase the level of competition among the churches for future new members. This probably would result in (1) a continued decrease in the number of congregations averaging 100 to 350 at worship, (2) an increase in the number averaging under 100 at worship as many congregations shrank in size, (3) a continued decrease in jobs, as pointed out earlier, for seminary graduates, (4) a continued erosion of denominational loyalties, (5) a doubling of highly attractive choices for churchgoers born after 1965 as they seek a church home in an increasingly consumer-driven society, and (6) a continued shift from denominational agencies to congregations and senior pastors as the primary building blocks for ecumenism.

WHO WILL BE THREATENED?

One argument against megachurches is that their numerical growth has been, and will be, at the expense of small congregations. That is a misreading of recent trends. Several denominations report an increase in the number of congregations reporting an average weekly worship attendance of fewer than 50 and in those averaging more than 1,000.

The tens of thousands of small Protestant congregations scattered across the North American continent serve a different constituency who bring a different set of expectations from the megachurch's constituency.

The tens of thousands of small Protestant congregations

199

scattered across the North American continent serve a different constituency who bring a different set of expectations from the megachurch's constituency. The churchgoers who place a high value on intimacy, simplicity, predictability, perpetuating local traditions, an attachment to a sacred place, kinship ties, and a geographical definition of community represent a different ecclesiastical market from the people who seek what the megachurch offers.

To be more precise, the least threatened congregations will include (1) the small house churches owned and operated by a corps of deeply dedicated volunteers; (2) the congregations averaging 25 to 60 at worship in which the ministerial responsibilities are fulfilled by trained volunteers or by bivocational pastors or retired clergy or by teams of volunteers from a megachurch that has adopted several small congregations as components of their network of off-campus ministries; (3) those smaller congregations that have developed a high-quality package of relevant ministries with a precisely defined constituency, such as home-schooling parents or couples in an intercultural marriage or first-generation immigrants; (4) the small single-cell congregation that is located in a sparsely populated community where the adult children of members can find attractive employment opportunities; (5) the congregations able to attract and keep a personable, energetic, highly competent, caring, extroverted, and creative pastor for a thirty- to forty-year pastorate; and (6) the small congregation organized around a clearly defined and distinctive doctrinal stance.

Those most threatened by an increase in the number of very large churches include (1) those very large churches organized primarily around the personality and preaching of an exceptionally attractive pulpiteer who resigns on moral charges after a decade or more of rapid numerical growth; (2) those congregations that were averaging 350 to 700 at worship but now offer irrelevant preaching, low-quality adult learning experiences, a youth program that repels teenagers, and severely limited pastoral care of members; (3) smaller congregations who want the services of a full-time, experienced, and fully credentialed resident pastor, but who are unable or unwilling to provide a total compensation package (housing, utilities, health insurance, cash salary, and pension) of at least $35,000 annually; (4) those congregations averaging 150 to 700 at worship that combine a functionally obsolete building on an inadequate site at a poor location with average-quality worship, below-average-quality learning opportunities for all ages, and a definition of "missions" based on sending dollars to hire others to do missions on our behalf; (5) those leaders who believe the best way to grow new megachurches is to plant heavily subsidized new missions that will be averaging 60 to 80 at worship by the end of the first year, 125 by the end of the third year, and will be fully self-supporting by the end of five years; (6) those congregations of all sizes that experience perpetual and divisive internal turmoil over disagreements on identity, role, personalities, social-justice issues, schedules, music, and the power of local traditions; (7) larger congregations that are experiencing a severe mismatch among the gifts, priorities, theological position, personality, and leadership style of the recently arrived successor to a long-tenured senior minister and what that congregation needs in this chapter of its history; and (8) the very large and numerically growing congregation that has outgrown its physical facilities, but cannot or will not relocate the meeting place.

In summary, a reasonable guess is that the number of small Protestant congregations will continue to increase with a growing proportion staffed with bivocational pastors while an increasing proportion of younger churchgoers will choose a very large congregation.

WHAT IS THE NEW ENTITLEMENT?

"My wife and I were married in June of 1946, and we joined Bethany Church the following September," recalled Ralph Olson, a longtime pillar of that congregation in a conversation with a staff member of the regional judicatory of the denomination. "About twelve years ago, you came out and told us we had three choices. We could try to plateau in size, which you warned probably would be the most difficult alternative to implement. Or we could watch passively as our members grew older in age and fewer in numbers. Or we could relocate to a large site and make a fresh start in new and modern facilities with adequate parking. As you know, we chose your third alternative. We purchased this twenty-six-acre site and have just completed our third building program. Our average worship attendance has nearly tripled from about 500 at the old location to nearly 1,500 last year. The two Saturday evening services run a combined total of about 600, and we have another 900 divided among the three Sunday morning services."

"That increase in attendance is impressive," commented the denominational staff person, "but equally important is that this congregation is at least twenty years younger than it was when you moved. As I recall our conversation, I suggested that if you wanted to reach younger generations, you needed more off-street parking."

"You called that one right!" affirmed Ralph. "In 1949 I was asked to serve on the property committee at Bethany, and I still remember the day three of us volunteered to put up the parking signs. We had a total of five spaces—one was reserved for the minister, two for first-time visitors, one for Mrs. Holland, who was in a wheelchair, and one for the Sunday school superintendent. Subsequently, we purchased three houses next door, cleared the land, built that educational wing, and paved enough of the rest for about sixty spaces of off-steet parking. Shortly after that, you met with us and warned that was not sufficient. At our new location, we have 500 spaces of off-street parking, and most of them are used at least once every Sunday morning. We have a lot of families that come to church in two different vehicles."

"That matches the experience of many other congregations," observed the denominational staffer. "If you want to reach people born after World War II, you need a surplus of off-street parking."

"My question today is on the same subject, but a different generation," continued Ralph. "You're right; our congregation today is much younger than it was at the old location. But we also are growing older. What do we have to do to reach larger numbers of the generations born after 1965? We have a lot of the so-called baby boomers, but we're short on younger adults. We have a surplus of off-street parking, but that doesn't seem to be the big attraction for today's younger adults."

"Let me give you two answers to what really is a complicated question," came the reply. "First of all, what you are describing is simply a product of the birth dearth of the 1965–80 era. The number of babies born each year drops by one-fourth when 1975 is compared to 1955. One out of four of the people you are trying to reach simply isn't there. They weren't born.

"A second response to your question can best be offered in historical terms," continued this denominational staffer. "Please understand that what I'm saying does oversimplify life, but it will lead us into your question. Long before I was born, the churches discovered that if they wanted to reach the generations born after 1890, they would have to bring electricity into their meetinghouses. This aroused widespread opposition, largely for health and safety reasons, but in less than fifty years, a church with electric lights went from being rare to being commonplace.

"The next two watersheds also were primarily real estate

issues," added this staffer. "The generations born after about 1920 wanted indoor plumbing. For most congregations, this meant running water in the church kitchen and a unisex closet that contained a toilet, wash basin, and mirror. More recently, the women born after about 1940 expect a large rest room resembling what is available in the enclosed shopping mall. It is worth noting that in the supermarkets constructed before 1980, rest rooms available to the public were concealed in the rear of the store and you had to ask directions to find them. The new supermarkets have easy-to-find and highly visible rest rooms, near the entrance from the parking lot. The other change is the one we've been talking about. If a church is serious about attracting the generations born after World War II, that usually requires a surplus of convenient and accessible off-street parking."

"I'm interested in your comments about rest rooms," interrupted Ralph. "At our old location, we had five rest rooms, and they contained a combined total of eleven toilets. In our new building, with three times as many worshipers on the weekend, we have twelve rest rooms with a total of fifty-four toilets. That includes the rest rooms in our big children's wing."

"Before we get to your question about new expectations, let me generalize about five other expectations younger generations have brought to the churches," continued this denominational staffer. "Many of those born after about 1950 came with a demand for a more relaxed dress code. We can see this most clearly among the male teachers from that generation in today's high schools and colleges, but also in the way people dress for church. I see an extremely relaxed dress code in most of our new missions designed to reach younger adults.

"Chronologically, the generations born after approximately 1955 concluded that the traditional presentation-type worship service was boring and irrelevant. One result has been an increasing number of churches that offer at least one nontraditional worship experience every weekend that speaks to them."

204

"Are you referring to contemporary worship?" asked Ralph.

"Yes, that's a word we hear a lot, but I prefer the more inclusive term 'nontraditional,' " came the reply. "Typically this can be described as more of a participatory style that is marked by its high energy level, by a fast pace, by a greater reliance on visual communication, and by a greater reliance on contemporary Christian music. It often also is described as a Spirit-filled experience.

"In addition, the younger the people in the room, the less likely worship will be led by talking heads. The talking heads gradually are disappearing from the network news on television and are being replaced by video scenes. A parallel pattern can be seen in preaching as the oral illustration is replaced by a video clip projected onto the screen. The cordless microphone means the person delivering the message no longer is confined to the pulpit but can walk around and create eye contact with scores of people."

"I know what you're describing," commented Ralph, "but a lot of folks from my generation prefer traditional worship with classical Christian music."

"Yes, that's true, and that raises a related issue. A lot of churchgoers want to be a part of an intergenerational congregation, but they want that church to be responsive to their expectations. The translation of that is choices. The greater the emphasis on an intergenerational constituency and the younger the congregation, the greater the demand for choices. This often means designing and offering three different worship experiences every weekend.

"Fourth, the generations born after about 1955 have produced the second biggest baby boom in American history. They come expecting that the church will offer attractive, high-quality, and relevant ministries with families with young children. One illustration of that is the easiest way to get a new mission off to a good start is through a heavy emphasis on children's ministries.

"Finally, many of the younger generations, especially those who have moved far away from both their kinfolk and their friends, hope they will find a sense of community in the church they choose. That wish may become a reality in the large congregations that are always creating new groups or those that identify themselves as a congregation of communities. In the vast majority of American Protestant congregations, however, that hope is not fulfilled. These single-cell churches that describe themselves as one big extended family frequently are perceived by newcomers as a closed circle. Unless you were born into it or marry into it or have an exceptionally high level of competence in pushing yourself into that closely knit fellowship, it is easy to remain a self-identified outsider. The disappearance of the geographically defined neighborhood church has made this a major concern. This helps to explain why the best of the new missions attract so many recent newcomers to that larger community."

"If I can summarize what you've said," reflected Ralph, "the first three big expectations new generations brought to the church concerned real estate. They were electric lights, indoor plumbing, and parking. The more recent expectations concerned worship and included a relaxed dress code, nontraditional worship with the disappearance of the talking heads, high-quality children's ministries, and the search for an open community that welcomes newcomers. What's the newest expectation?"

"That's a reasonably fair summary, and we now can move on to the expectation many of the adults born during the last third of the century bring to church. Before I describe it, Ralph, you need to understand that churchgoers do not expect to be billed individually for the cost of electricity. They do not expect to find pay toilets in the church, and they do not expect to feed the parking meters in church parking lots. This new expectation, which is not universal and evokes considerable opposition, is that high-quality and free child care will be

206

available when they come to church. That includes Sunday morning worship, Thursday evening choir rehearsal, Monday evening adult Bible study, Wednesday evening programming, the Thursday morning meeting of the women's missionary society, Tuesday evening committee meetings, and every other time volunteers come to the church."

"We didn't expect that when our kids were young," objected Ralph. "We felt that if you wanted to be a parent, you should accept the responsibilities of looking after your own children. We staffed the nursery with volunteers on Sunday morning. If several members of the chancel choir brought their kids to choir rehearsal, they chipped in a dollar each to hire a baby-sitter. Why should we now be expected to help pay for the child care of someone else's kids?"

"You really have two choices," came the reply. "One is to restrict membership to adults whose youngest child is at least twelve years of age. The other is to affirm the fact that new generations bring new expectations."

"Sounds to me more like they see free baby-sitting as an entitlement, not as an expectation," grumbled Ralph. "What's next on the list of expectations people will bring to church?"

"I'm not sure," replied the denominational staffer, "and one is not really new; it simply is less widely ignored than it was. This is better training for volunteers. For a long time now, society has been teaching people that graduation from law school or medical school or business school or engineering school does not prepare you to go out and practice that profession. It only prepares you to enter the postgraduate training you need to be a successful practitioner. We once thought that the vows of membership prepared a person to be an effective volunteer in the church. We now recognize that training can help. More important, younger generations bring an assumption that they benefit from a training program designed specifically for Sunday school teachers or board members or trustees or youth counselors or leaders of a prayer group or for teaching an adult Bible study group or for evangelists or for new parents or for newlyweds or for calling on the bereaved. The younger generations believe they are entitled to the appropriate training required for the volunteer role they have been asked to fill.

"A second one also is here and is illustrated by your new building. In the 1980s you folks built a three-story addition to that old Bethany Church building. One of the reasons you decided to relocate the meeting place was the need for more parking. Another was the discontent with that three-story building. You now meet in a modern one-story building. Except where the cost or availability of land rules this out, churchgoers of all ages have come to agree that this is a one-story world. The church basement disappeared many years ago. Now, except for rooms for children and youth, the second story is becoming a relic from the past.

"A third expectation, which runs through much of what we've been talking about, is that each new generation that comes along expects higher quality. A highly visible example is the quality of the rest rooms. More important is the quality of communication or the quality of the child care or the quality of the group life."

"I'm still hung up on your suggestions that we should provide high-quality, free child care whenever volunteers come to the church," reflected Ralph. "My offhand calculations are that would add somewhere between $20,000 and $30,000 a year to our budget. I simply can't see that happening anytime soon."

"It may not happen next year, or even the year after that," agreed this denominational staffer. "Remember, it took fifty years between when electric lights were first introduced and when they became the norm in nearly every church. It was thirty years from the time people began to drive to church in their automobiles and when we began to provide paved off-street parking lots."

"I guess maybe we're talking about several dozen funerals," conceded Ralph, "and maybe mine will be one of them."

CONGREGATIONS OR COMMUNITIES?

For this discussion, the very large congregations can be divided into four groups. The smallest consists of those that perceive themselves to be one large worshiping community. While it is the smallest of these three groups today, as recently as the 1950s it was the dominant pattern among the very large churches. The ideal is that the entire constituency will gather in the same room at the same time for the corporate worship of God. Today this frequently is not possible because of limitations of parking or of seats in the sanctuary, and so the same worship experience is offered two or three times on Sunday morning. One of the operating assumptions is that there is a high degree of homogeneity within that constituency. A second is the need for a very large room for worship. A third is that one minister will be responsible for most of the preaching.

A second, and larger group, perceive themselves to be a congregation of classes, choirs, cells, circles, fellowships, and organizations. "I'm part of the 9:30 service, so I attend an adult class at 10:45 on Sunday morning." "My wife and I always go to the eleven o'clock service because we prefer more traditional worship. She also sings in the choir at that service." "Most of our friends go to the early service at 8:15, so that's the one we have chosen. And we stick around for our adult class, which begins at 9:30."

That weekend schedule may include one or two worship experiences on Saturday evening, two or three different services on Sunday morning, one late Sunday afternoon, and perhaps one on Monday evening. The Sunday morning schedule may include one traditional worship service, one nontraditional service, and one that is described as "blended."

Each service requires its own bulletin, which often includes special announcements for that particular constituency. Most of the regular attendees identify with a particular service at a specific time. For many, their *secondary* identification is with a choir or class or some other group. The operational assumption is that choices are necessary to respond effectively to the high degree of diversity within the constituency.

A third group of very large churches conceptualize themselves as a congregation of congregations of classes, choirs, circles, and so on.

The fourth, and what appears to be the most rapidly growing group, consists of the very large churches that perceive themselves as a congregation of communities. The *primary* identification of a majority of the constituency is with a smaller community within that large collection of people. Perhaps the most common example is the member of the chancel choir who never misses either choir rehearsal or Sunday morning worship from late August through June, but is absent on four of the eight summer weekends when the chancel choir is on vacation. More numerous are those whose primary loyalty is to an adult Sunday school class or to a circle in the women's fellowship or to an early morning weekday Bible study/prayer group that meets in an office building or to a Thursday evening mutual support group for those involved in a traumatic divorce experience or to other members of a three- to five-person mission team leading a new off-campus ministry or with other active participants in a social justice ministry or to a task force to help alleviate world hunger or to an instrumental group in the ministry of music or to that weekly luncheon gathering of senior citizens or to a church-sponsored softball team.

In retrospect, it appears that the "one big congregation" self-identification was more popular in the 1950–80 era than in recent years. That self-identification led to the construction of huge worship centers seating between 1,000 and 6,000 worshipers. It also undergirded the assumption that a big congregation needed one excellent preacher.

The affirmation of diversity and the pressures of being sensitive and responsive to the expectations of new generations of churchgoers was a major factor in motivating congregational leaders to conceptualize themselves as a congregation of congregations. The growing popularity of contemporary Christian music added impetus to this trend. This has led to a sharp increase in the number of worship experiences offered on the weekend (with many large churches offering concurrent Sunday morning worship services, some of which may be off-campus), the construction of smaller worship centers (many of which are multipurpose) seating 200 to 700 worshipers, and a recognition of the need for two or three highly competent preachers on the staff.

A more sophisticated version of the congregation of congregations is reflected in this comment: "In the typical month, approximately 2,000 different people worship with us at least once. About 1,400 of them are regular attenders and also participate on a weekly basis in one or more of our other ministries. Out of that 1,400, about 800 either have chosen to take the vows of membership or are enrolled in a yearlong weekly class for potential future members. Out of that 800, nearly 300 have completed our training program that is designed to transform believers into disciples. Slightly more than half of those 300 have completed the appropriate training program required to enable them to be productive leaders in ministry."

The clearest expression of the self-identified congregation of communities can be seen in scores of multigenerational and multicultural megachurches that are multisite ventures. This small worshiping community meets in a storefront on Sunday morning and worships in Vietnamese. That one has leased a store in a strip mall and is composed largely of upper-middle-class Anglos in the 25-35 age bracket who, back when they were teenagers, were "turned off" by the traditional institutional expression of the church. A third congregation worships in the community room of a large apartment complex largely occupied by single-parent mothers and their children. A fourth meets in the seventy-year-old sanctuary early Sunday morning for a worship service centered on Holy Communion. Most of those worshipers are past age 60, and their ties to one another are reinforced by weekday ministry opportunities. A fifth community is a group of nearly 300 formerly married and never-married adults in the 35-55 age bracket who gather for three or four hours every Friday evening for a meal, fellowship, and learning, but scatter among various opportunities for worship. A sixth community is an adult Sunday school class with an average attendance of nearly 300 that meets in the middle hour on Sunday morning and is taught in a lecture-and-question format by a minister on the staff. Some of them worship before class at one of the two concurrent services at the first hour, while others worship at the late service. A seventh community gathers for worship at the first hour in a Spanish-language service led by a pastor on the staff who was born and educated in Colombia. An eighth community consists of the American-born children of Korean-born parents who worship in English (one-fourth of them are married to an American-born spouse of Western European descent) on Saturday evening. The Sunday mid-morning service is organized around contemporary Christian music, a high level of spontaneity, laughter, applause, intercessory prayer, and visual communication and attracts many adults born after 1965 who have a primary allegiance to one of the other subgroups or communities.

This model affirms the need for at least two, and preferably three, different rooms that can be used for the corporate worship of God. This is in addition to somewhere between 1 and 200 off-campus meeting places. One may be the sanctuary constructed many years ago; one may be the gymnasium or the fellowship hall; and one may be a chapel. In a few megachurches, a new worship service is scheduled to begin every 15 or 30 minutes in order to facilitate the flow of traffic in the parking lot. Few question the need for at least three preachers on at least fifty weekends of the year.

Which of these three models will be the dominant one among the megachurches of 2030? Which model represents your congregation? If you reply, "We include a piece of all three," which model represents the one you are moving toward and which is the one that is shrinking?

Which model is God calling your congregation to implement? This last question should be answered before you begin to design new facilities for worship and before you begin to redefine the staff configuration for the twenty-first century!

WHAT ARE THE UNIQUE ASSETS OF THE MEGACHURCH?

In a provocative and thoughtful analysis of what people expect from church, Robert L. Randall suggests people come to a church with a four-point agenda. They come with:

1. Yearnings to feel understood.
2. Yearnings to understand.
3. Yearnings to belong.
4. Yearnings for hope.[6]

All four yearnings reflect relationships, not functions or tasks. This is where the small-membership congregation has an advantage, since it naturally tends to be organized around relationships, not tasks or functions or obligations.

The Christian gospel, however, provides the foundation and resources for every worshiping community, regardless of size, to respond effectively to all four of those expectations if the people want to do that. A creative effort may require training in evangelism, in listening skills, in Bible study, in interpersonal relationships, and in decision making, but those experiences are all within the realm of the possible. One megachurch may have advantages in terms of available resources, but it does not have a monopoly!

Nearly all very large congregations averaging 800 or more at worship, however, do enjoy three advantages that can be called unique. The first of these, which has been referred to earlier in this book, is that very large churches usually can mobilize the resources necessary to offer a broad range of choices. That provides more possibilities to feel understood, more opportunities to gain understanding, more places and groups to strengthen the sense of belonging, and more experiences to undergird hope.

. . . the most distinctive, of these assets is that most very large congregations have learned how to "do big church." Many of the policies and practices that are appropriate for nineteen out of twenty congregations turn out to be counterproductive when followed in the very large churches.

This can be seen most clearly in those megachurches that are designed as a congregation of congregations of choirs, circles, cells, classes, fellowships, groups, and organizations or a congregation of communities.

The second unique asset of the megachurch is the high ceiling on what can be accomplished. The vast majority of congregations in American Protestantism operate with a limited inventory of assets. This often means "creaming off" the most gifted and the most committed volunteers to focus on institutional maintenance and staffing the administrative machinery. Likewise, the lack of resources tends to place a low ceiling on

214

dreams, hopes, and goals. It is easier to dream big dreams when there is an abundance of resources, including many gifted volunteers.

The third, and the most distinctive, of these assets is that most very large congregations have learned how to "do big church." Many of the policies and practices that are appropriate for nineteen out of twenty congregations turn out to be counterproductive when followed in the very large churches. The most highly visible expression of this distinctive asset consists of two patterns. One is the small but growing number of megachurches that have accepted the role of a teaching church. These congregations invite people to come and see what we are doing, to discover how and why we do what we do, and to learn from our failures as well as from our successes.

The second pattern consists of that growing number of congregational leaders, both lay and clergy, who arrange their schedules to spend two or three or more days annually with a teaching church. These leaders believe that if their congregation is to achieve its potential, it will be more productive to learn from the experiences of big churches than to study how small and middle-sized congregations carry out their ministries.

More subtle, but at least equally significant, is the strategy to be followed in planting new missions. One model calls for encouraging congregations averaging 100 to 700 at worship to sponsor new missions. A natural tendency is to attempt to clone the sponsoring congregation. That usually produces a new mission that plateaus in size as a small or middle-sized congregation. An overlapping model is to assign a minister with five to thirty years' experience as the pastor of small and middle-sized congregations to serve as the founding pastor of that new mission. The usual result is the new mission plateaus in size with an average worship attendance of 350 or fewer.

A radically different model begins with creating a staff of three to five paid staff members, plus three to ten lay volun-

215

teers, all of whom have had at least five years' experience in a megachurch. They know how to "do big church." This is the model that is used if the goal is to average at least 300 in worship attendance by the end of the first year and 700 by the end of the third or fourth year.

A parallel can be seen in the congregation averaging 450 to 700 at worship that has the potential to double in size. When the time comes to seek a successor to the departing senior minister, in broad general terms, they have three choices.

1. To choose a successor who is a young, promising, and attractive minister and who has been effective in serving congregations averaging 150 to 300 at worship. That requires the new senior minister (a) to learn the culture of this particular congregation, (b) to unlearn what worked so well in the smaller congregation averaging 150 to 300 at worship, and (c) to discover how to "do big church."

... the most significant export the megachurch can make is how to fulfill the role of a very large congregation.

2. To invite the senior associate minister of a megachurch to become the new senior minister. Presumably that individual knows how to "do big church" and has only to learn the distinctive culture, personality, and current role of this congregation.

3. To anticipate the future by calling, at least five to seven years before the departure of that senior minister, an associate pastor who has spent at least five years on the staff of a very large congregation. Presumably that associate minister has learned how to "do big church" and also fully understands the distinctive culture of this congregation. The big learning for this new senior minister is how to be an effective senior minister.

In summary, the most significant export the megachurch can make is how to fulfill the role of a very large congregation. One way to do that is to accept the role as a self-identified teaching church. A second is to sponsor new missions that have the potential to grow into very large congregations. A third is to enlist and train leaders, both paid staff and volunteers, who carry with them the wisdom of how to "do big church" when they depart to become leaders in other worshiping communities.

GENERATIONS AND VALUES

The health, vitality, and numerical growth of tens of thousands of churches back in the 1950s were fed by the generations born in the first three decades of the twentieth century. Tom Brokaw, the television anchor for NBC, refers more precisely to the people born shortly before and after 1920. (In generational terms, the babies born in the 1914–28 era.) He concluded that this was "the greatest generation any society has produced."[7]

Brokaw contends that this was the last generation who affirmed the values conveyed in such words as *duty, honor, country, flag, patriotism, family, church, faith, loyalty, self-sacrifice, purpose, modesty,* and *responsibility.*

That may represent one more effort at an excessive romanticizing of the past, but it does illustrate the congruence between the values taught by the churches in the 1950s and the values churchgoers had been taught since childhood. The expectations people brought to church were compatible with the values propagated by the churches.

One of the big unknowns about the future concerns the value systems of the generations born in the last quarter of the twentieth century. What will be the most influential differences between the value systems of those born in the 1910–28 era and those born in the post-1975 era? What will be in the rule books they bring to church?

> . . . many in the younger generations have replaced loyalty and self-sacrifice with self-determination.

One example, to go back to Brokaw's list, is that many in the younger generations have replaced loyalty and self-sacrifice with self-determination. Younger generations find it relatively easy to switch from one religious tradition to a different one. In recent years, several denominations have redefined their priorities from resourcing congregations to regulating ministerial and congregational practices.[8] This has motivated younger adults to leave and go to a religious tradition that affirms a high level of trust in local leadership.[9] This value on self-determination also can be seen in church finances. Members born in the first third of the twentieth century expressed their loyalty by willingly sending money to denominational headquarters where decisions would be made on how those dollars would be allocated. Younger generations are more likely to respond generously to requests for designated giving where they can determine the ultimate destination of their financial contributions.

Will the value systems of the younger generations provide a supportive or hostile societal environment for the megachurch in the twenty-first century? By 2030, we should have an answer to that question.

CHAPTER EIGHT

A Denominational Perspective

The second half of the twentieth century saw the number of nongovernmental organizations (N.G.O.s) accredited by the United Nations increase from 41 in 1948 to more than 1,500 in 1998. One of them, the International Campaign to Ban Land Mines, and its founder, Jodi Williams, were awarded the Nobel Peace Prize in 1997. Between September 1993 and January 1996 the government of Angola paid $40 million a year to Executive Outcome, a private military company, to arm and train 5,000 soldiers.[1] Four N.G.O.s (CARE, World Vision International, Save the Children Federation, and Oxfam Federation) together disburse one-fifth of the $10 billion spent annually on disaster relief and to help refugees.[2] The Ford Foundation partially financed the settlement of the civil war in El Salvador. During the civil disorder in Chiapas, Mexico, in the late 1990s, 276 N.G.O.s sent a combined total of 4,500 foreigners to that tiny part of the planet. N.G.O.s have become a major rival to the United Nations in the conduct of international relations.

For 300 years, from the Treaty of Westphalia to the middle of this century, nation-states were the building blocks for international relations. The League of Nations and the United Nations both were organized on the assumption that nation-states represented the basic organizational units for the contemporary political world. (This has turned out to be a fallacious assumption in African countries where tribal allegiances often are far stronger than loyalties to a national government.) One scholar recently commented, "As governments downsize and new challenges crowd the international agenda, N.G.O.s fill the breach."[3] The pressure is on every major world power, including France, Russia, the United States, Great Britain, and Japan, to reconsider what it can and cannot do. Every vacuum created by these reappraisals is ripe to be filled by an N.G.O.

N.G.O.s also have become powerful voices in shaping public opinion and in influencing the decisions of governments.[4]

A parallel trend can be seen in the role of denominational systems in American Protestantism. Two hundred years after the Treaty of Westphalia it was clear the denominations provided the institutional context for American Protestantism. Their power and influence continued to grow and probably peaked in the 1960s and 1970s.

The National Council of the Churches of Christ in the U.S.A. was founded in 1950 and now includes 34 member communions. It came into existence in an era when no one questioned the role of national denominational systems as the basic building blocks for ecumenism just as nation-states were accepted as the constituency for the United Nations.

. . . that first wave of mid-twentieth-century parachurch organizations focused on evangelistic efforts to reach younger generations with the gospel of Jesus Christ.

Back in the 1940s, however, the ecclesiastical equivalents of the N.G.O. began to become increasingly visible. These frequently are referred to as parachuch organizations.[5] While several highly influential parachurch groups were created in the nineteenth century (The American Bible Society in 1816, American Sunday School Union in 1824, American Tract Society in 1825, and the Young Men's Christian Association in

1844), the big wave did not begin until the 1930s. Inter-Varsity, the Navigators, Campus Crusade for Christ, Youth for Christ, Young Life, Teen Challenge, Fellowship of Christian Athletes, and the Institute in Basic Youth Conflict are among the better known.

To a substantial degree that first wave of mid-twentieth-century parachurch organizations focused on evangelistic efforts to reach younger generations with the gospel of Jesus Christ. The denominational agencies continued to service their congregations and to maintain their institutions, most of which were created in the nineteenth century, while the parachurch groups focused their evangelistic efforts on individuals born in the middle of the twentieth century. The two big areas of overlap and competition were (1) ministries with high school and university students and (2) providing printed resources for Sunday schools and other study groups.

THE NEW COMPETITORS

More recently an increasing number of parachurch organizations have been competing directly with denominational agencies. Examples include (1) counsel in congregational capital fund campaigns; (2) publications; (3) training experiences for volunteers; (4) conflict resolution; (5) evaluation of staff; (6) litigation; (7) spiritual growth retreats; (8) parish consultations; (9) continuing education experiences for pastors and program staff; (10) resources for adult Bible study programs; (11) youth rallies; (12) campus ministries; (13) specialized ministries with adults in jail or prison; (14) social justice issues; (15) enlisting, sending, and supporting Christian missionaries in other countries; (16) training church planters; (17) resourcing home-schooling parents; (18) providing training experiences and a network for intentional interim pastors; (19) mobilizing resources for the relief of victims of natural disasters; and (20) the design of congregational web sites on the Internet.

221

TWO NEW KIDS ON THE BLOCK

For those interested in the life, ministry, and future of the megachurch, the first of two symbolically significant events came in the mid-1980s. With the notable exception of the Board for Homeland Ministries of the United Church of Christ, most of the larger denominations ignored the needs of the senior pastors of very large congregations. One reason why was their assumption that these were resource-rich congregations that did not have any unmet needs. Another was that the system for representation at regional and national conventions called for representing institutions (congregations), not people. One result was an underrepresentation of the people in the very large congregations. That naturally led to the focusing of denominational resources on the 60 percent of the congregations that include one-fourth of the people.

Many of these ministers were hungry for the opportunity to socialize, to reflect on common concerns, and to network with senior pastors of other megachurches.

An unanticipated consequence of being ignored was the increased feeling of alienation between the leaders in the very large congregations and their denominational systems. Many of these leaders, both clergy and lay, felt they were being neglected, exploited, ignored, overlooked, and unduly criticized. At the typical regional pastors' meeting, the senior ministers of the very large churches, who accounted for approximately 2 percent of the clergy in the room, left convinced that their agendas had little to no overlap with the concerns being addressed by their denominational leaders. One response was to stay away from the next meeting.

Concurrently, the number of nondenominational or independent megachurches was increasing. Many of these ministers were hungry for the opportunity to socialize, to reflect on common concerns, and to network with senior pastors of other megachurches.

Two Texans with a telephone and a post office box in Tyler, Texas, discovered the vacuum and in 1985 created a new parachurch organization, the Leadership Network, to respond to this unmet need. The enthusiastic participation of literally hundreds of senior ministers of megachurches validated the need for this new parachurch organization. The Leadership Network has been able to respond effectively to needs that no one denomination could meet unilaterally.

The second came in 1990–91 when a group of senior pastors of megachurches gathered to create Churches Uniting in Global Mission (CUGM). CUGM is a network of senior ministers from several religious traditions, including mainline Protestant denominations, charismatic churches, independent congregations, and Holiness bodies. CUGM represents five significant contemporary trends. First, it is the creation of and is administered by senior pastors of very large congregations. It is not a council of congregations. It is not a coalition or federation or council of denominations.

Second, the central organizing principle is the focus on evangelism and missions, not on doctrine or denominational allegiance or ecumenism or ethnicity or language or a specific social-justice issue or a common Western European religious heritage or the geographical proximity of the participants. Third, the participants come with resources to be allocated to missions and evangelism. They do not come with needs that they hope someone else will resource. Unlike many cooperative arrangements that bring congregations together around weaknesses, CUGM is organized around strength. The operational principle is to identify and validate unmet needs and to build the coalition that can mobilize the resources to meet those needs. Fourth, CUGM does not attempt to be all-inclusive. It clearly is a Christ-centered religious movement. Fifth, CUGM draws a disproportionately large number of its participants from west of the Mississippi River. That contrasts with the fact that the majority of the American population, the majority of national denominational staff members, and the majority of Protestant congregations are located east of that great river. New approaches to ministries often enjoy a more supportive environment in the West than exists in the East.

The Leadership Network and CUGM illustrate the continuing attraction of very large congregations to parachurch movements. That, combined with the growing number of nondenominational megachurches, raises a question about the future role of denominational systems. Before discussing that issue, however, it may be instructive to look at the recent record of one denomination.

A CASE STUDY

The Evangelical Covenant Church of America traces its history back to immigrants from Sweden in the last quarter of the nineteenth century. By the end of 1997 it included 650 congregations (up from 596 in 1991) with a combined confirmed membership of 93,136 and a combined average worship attendance for five Sundays in November and December of 113,937. (The Covenanters project high expectations of members.)

In 1990 the largest Covenant congregation reported an average worship attendance of 2,271 for those five autumn weekends. Seven years later, the largest congregation was averaging 4,756 at worship and ten (1.6 percent of all congregations) reported an average worship attendance of 800 or more. For the denomination as a whole, 4 percent of the 650 congregations accounted for 23 percent of the total attendance and 28 percent of the net growth in attendance since

1990. In 1997 the five largest churches reported a combined worship attendance of 11,541, up from 6,578 for the five largest in 1990. The number with a worship attendance of 1,000 or more increased from 2 in 1990 to 4 in 1994 to 6 in 1997. Fifteen of the 25 largest Covenant churches in 1990 were still among the largest 25 seven years later. Six of the largest 25 in 1997 either did not exist in 1990 or were averaging under 400 at worship.

The experiences of this middle-sized denomination illustrate several contemporary trends: (1) The number of very large congregations continues to increase; (2) a tiny percentage of all congregations accounts for a large proportion of churchgoers; (3) the numerically growing denominations tend to be found among those religious traditions that project high expectations of people, that are experiencing an increase in the number of congregations, and that are encouraging the emergence of more very large congregations; (4) the size required to be the largest congregation within a particular denomination has doubled in recent years; (5) very large congregations are fragile institutions (10 of the 25 largest Covenant churches in 1990 were not on the list of the largest 25 only seven years later); (6) a relatively few very large congregations and a few new missions often account for most of the net numerical growth within a denomination; and (7) the number required to be classified as "large" keeps increasing (for the Covenant

What is the most effective approach to creating and undergirding a strong denominational system? To welcome, include, and build on islands of strength and health? Or to focus on the numerically shrinking congregations . . . ?

from 542 average worship attendance in 1990 to 580 in 1997).

This case study also introduces an extremely important ideological question: What is the most effective approach to creating and undergirding a strong denominational system? To welcome, include, and build on islands of strength and health? Or to focus on the numerically shrinking congregations, to overrepresent (in proportion to their membership) delegates and leaders from small congregations, and to grant substantial authority to representatives from the small congregations to decide on the priorities in the expenditure of denominational funds, most of which come from a small number of very large churches?

COUNTERPRODUCTIVE TACTICS

Another way to state the same basic issue is to ask, What are the most effective components of a strategy designed to undermine the health and vitality of a denominational system? The historical record suggests that among the most influential are these:

1. Let highly divisive social and political issues such as ecumenism, the role of women in congregational life, homosexuality, abortion, euthanasia, vouchers for elementary school children, American foreign policy, and political correctness dominate the agenda at the annual denominational meeting.

2. Cut back as close to zero as possible in new church development, or if that is not possible, use a small-church model in designing new missions.

3. Place high on the priority list in the allocation of scarce resources those concerns in which that denomination has experienced a high failure rate in past years.

4. Move in the direction of increasing the level of theological pluralism within that denominational tradition.

226

5. Alienate the senior pastors of the very large congregations from that denominational system.

6. Cut back on the number of congregations averaging more than 500 at worship.

7. Reinforce the distrust of congregational leaders by adopting additional rules and regulations governing congregational practices, organizational structures, priorities, and decision making.

8. Drop missions and evangelism to the second or third level of priorities in the allocation of scarce denominational resources.

9. Place a floor on the number of dollars each congregation is expected to send to the denominational headquarters every year. (These floors are usually perceived by congregational leaders to be ceilings.)

10. Underrepresent, in proportion to their membership, the very large congregations in choosing volunteer leaders for denominational boards and committees.

11. Encourage short pastorates of seven years or less.

12. Encourage large congregations seeking a new senior minister to choose someone now serving a smaller congregation.

13. Discourage the emergence of self-identified teaching churches.

14. Encourage both long-established and numerically shrinking churches and new missions to become dependent on long-term (three years or longer) denominational financial subsidies.

15. Encourage two or more numerically shrinking churches to merge and become one congregation.

16. In designing the system for the redistribution of money, create one that rewards numerical shrinkage and/or poor stewardship and punishes numerical growth and good stewardship.

17. Place a high priority on the possibility of an eventual merger with one or more other denominations.

227

18. Define the primary responsibility of congregations as that of supporting denominational initiatives rather than defining the primary role of denominational agencies as resourcing congregations.

SHAPING THE FUTURE

What is the future of your denomination? One response is to ask how many of the eighteen items on this checklist for undermining a denomination are among the current operational policies of your religious tradition. How many can be documented by your denominational rule book? A more productive approach may be to ask these questions:

1. Will your denomination be able to enlist an adequate number of exceptionally high-quality candidates for the parish ministry from among the children born in the 1980–2010 era?

2. Will the post-high school training provided for these candidates prepare them to be effective pastors and program staffers in the twenty-first century? Will they be equipped to lead congregations in carryng out their basic purposes? (See question 21 in chapter 9.)

3. Will your denomination be able to design a strategy to plant the number and variety of new missions required to reach and serve new generations of American-born residents and recent immigrants? A maintenance goal is that the number of new missions will be equivalent to 1 percent of the current number of congregations in that denomination. A growth goal is 2 percent. The goal of becoming a multicultural denomination probably will require the equivalent of 3 percent.

4. Will your denomination double or triple the number of very large congregations? A modest goal would be for 2 percent of all congregations to average 800 or more at worship.

5. If the current thinking calls for the denomination to regulate congregational life and practices, can that be changed to expressing greater trust in local leadership, thereby unleashing a pool of creativity? What will be the number-one source of creativity? Denominational agencies? Or congregational leaders?[6]

Can your denominational system adopt as a guiding principle Clint Bolick's conclusion, "Time and again, when people are given greater power and responsibility over their lives they respond in remarkable fashion"?[7]

6. What will be the priorities in the allocation of scarce denominational resources (staff time and creativity, money, volunteers, etc.)? Will the two top priorities be (a) helping congregations design and implement ministry plans to reach and serve new constituencies and (b) identifying and building on islands of health and strength by giving birth to the new? Will the bottom of that list of priorities in the allocation of scarce resources include (a) extending the life of dying institutions a little longer, (b) subsidizing denominational institutions created in 1970 and earlier that could and should be financially self-supporting, and (c) replicating ministries that were effective in reaching and serving the generation born in the 1910–28 era in the expectation that these models also will be effective in reaching and serving the generations born after 1965?

7. Will the emergence of more megachurches be perceived as a threat? Or as a valuable resource?

8. Will congregations be encouraged to send money to denominational headquarters to be used in denominationally initiated missional ventures? Or will congregations be encouraged to initiate new missional efforts and to mobilize both volunteers and money to invest in these initiatives?

9. Will the denominational emphasis in enlisting and training a new generation of parish pastors and program staff members be primarily on (a) full-time ordained generalists or (b) full-time and part-time lay specialists?

SIX FORK-IN-THE-ROAD DECISIONS

An overlapping perspective for reflecting on the future of denominational systems is to look at several fork-in-the-road questions. Each one can become a self-fulfilling prophecy.

1. Will regional and national denominational agencies place a higher priority on resourcing congregations? Or will they, largely by default, encourage congregations to turn to parachurch organizations and teaching churches in their search for resources?

Will the denominational system be organized primarily to regulate the practices of congregations or primarily to resource congregational life and outreach? What does your denominational rule book emphasize?

2. Will the denominational systems focus on (a) challenging congregations to identify their God-given potential in ministry and resource congregations in fulfilling that potential or (b) encouraging congregations to provide the resources required to implement denominationally initiated programs and goals?

3. Will the denomination place a high priority on the redistribution of resources by asking the strong congregations to share their resources with the weak? Or will that high priority be given to challenging resource-rich congregations to undertake new ventures in ministry?

4. In the quest for funds, will the denominational systems focus largely on asking congregations to send money to headquarters, or will they look to individuals, family foundations, corporations, governmental agencies, and other nonprofit bodies as their number-one source of money?

5. Will congregations or senior ministers of large churches or pastors in general or regional judicatories or national denominational bodies or the independent churches be perceived as the crucial partners in the new wave of ecumenism?

6. How high a priority will the denomination give to

encouraging and helping those congregations now averaging 450 to 700 at worship to double or triple or quadruple in size? Will that rank above or below allocating resources to new church development or to designing and implementing new denominational initiatives or to helping numerically shrinking small and middle-sized congregations survive or to maintaining denominationally related institutions founded before 1970?

The answers to these and related questions will be shaped by what the policy makers believe the future will bring to American Christianity. Has the time come to prepare a new edition of your denominational rule book?

CHAPTER NINE

What Do You Believe?

Is your congregation a megachurch? Or does it possess the potential to grow into a megachurch? Do you believe that the Lord is calling your congregation to adopt the role and responsibilities of a megachurch? Or are you convinced that the recent emergence of so many megachurches is a threat to most existing congregations, and perhaps even to the institutional expression of Christianity in North America? Or do you believe that this is a passing fad that will be largely forgotten by the middle of the twenty-first century?

A useful beginning point for any group of congregational, or denominational, leaders responsible for planning for the early years of the third millennium can be to reach agreement on the context for ministry. If this group of leaders can agree on (1) the central components of the changing context for ministry, (2) the unique identity and role God is calling their faith community to accept in the years ahead, and (3) a reasonably accurate description of contemporary reality in your congregation or denomination, it will be easier to design and agree on a ministry plan for the next several years.

Beliefs, expectations, and convictions about what the future will bring shape our responses to immediate questions and issues. What do you believe?

1. The average (mean) size of a Christian congregation in the United States tripled during the twentieth century. Do you believe that will turn out to be the first stage of a long-term trend? Or do you believe that was a passing phenomenon and the size of the average Protestant congregation will shrink during the twenty-first century?

2. Today approximately 7 percent of all Protestant congregations account for nearly one-third of all American Protestant worshipers on the typical weekend. Do you believe that by 2050 the distribution will be that 10 percent of the churches will include one-half of the worshipers? Or that 10 percent will include fewer than one-third?

3. During the 1990s it became apparent that a disproportionately large number of the churchgoers born after 1950 could be found in the very large congregations. Do you believe this trend will continue? Or do you believe that as these younger generations grow older, they will seek out smaller churches? Do you believe the younger adults of 2030 will prefer small churches or very large congregations?

4. In the 1950s the first contact between a potential future member and a particular congregation usually was on Sunday morning. In the 1990s that first contact between a megachurch and a potential future constituent was more likely to be other than Sunday morning. That initial contact could be a wedding or an exercise class or a church-sponsored soccer game or a television program or a Tuesday evening mutual support group or a Saturday morning Bible study/prayer group or a web site or a memorial service or a Wednesday evening youth event or a Saturday evening worship service or an event sponsored by a social justice task force or a Thursday morning Bible study group meeting in an office building or a Christian day school or a parenting class or Monday evening worship.

What do you believe will be the circumstances for the majority of those initial first contacts in the twenty-first century?

5. The erosion of inherited institutional loyalties, the replacement of the neighborhood parish by the regional church, the increase in the number of interfaith and interdenominational marriages, the decrease in the number of adults who marry someone from their neighborhood, the power of consumerism, and the greater geographical separation of the place of work, the place of shopping, the place of recreation, and the place of worship from the place of residence have combined to raise the level of competition among the churches in reaching newcomers to the community and new generations of residents. Do you believe this level of competition will decrease? Or increase?

As more and more churchgoers shop for a new church home when they change their place of residence or when they become discontented with their present congregation, what do you believe is the minimum size for a congregation to be competitive? An average worship attendance of 135? 350? 500? 700? 800? 1,000? 1,500? 1,800? 3,500? 5,000?

6. The generations born after World War II project greater expectations on the church than was true of the generations born before 1930. That list includes choices in worship, a surplus of off-street parking, one-story buildings, air-conditioning, caterers, paid staff to do what formerly was done by volunteers, visual communication, help in the rearing of children, choices in learning, designated giving, high-quality child care, marriage enrichment retreats, and relevant training experiences for volunteers. Do you believe that the expectations brought by the churchgoers born in the 1980–2010 era will be even greater than those of their parents' generation?

7. What is sometimes described as "The Fourth Great Religious Reawakening in America" is a factor behind the recent emergence of a growing number of very large nondenominational congregations that are reaching a substantial proportion of the churchgoers born after 1955. A common characteristic of these churches is a high level of trust in local leadership. The smaller ones tend to be highly democratic and congregational in governance. The larger ones usually follow a representative system in which five to forty lay elders plus one or two or three ministers have been authorized to make most or all of the decisions on doctrine, priorities, schedule, real estate, staffing, biblical interpretation, missions, and worship. Do you believe this to be a significant trend? Or do you believe that in the twenty-first century churchgoers will want denominations to serve as regulatory bodies?

8. In the 1950s most Protestant congregations turned to their denominational system in the quest for resources. By the 1970s more and more congregations were turning to parachurch organizations for resources. The 1990s saw the emergence of the self-identified teaching church as a significant source of resources for congregational leaders. What will be the three most widely used sources of help and resources for congregations in the early years of the twenty-first century? Will the top three include (a) national denominational agencies, (b) regional denominational judicatories, (c) theological schools, (d) parachurch organizations, (e) teaching churches, (f) state universities, (g) church-related colleges and universities, (h) councils of churches, (i) independent retreat centers, (j) nonprofit publishing houses, (k) for-profit resource centers, (l) a loose network of independent entrepreneurs, (m) Christian missionaries coming to the United States from other continents, (n) coalitions of nonprofit institutions including congregations, (o) ministerial associations, or (p) ???

9. For most of American church history, it was widely assumed that a Protestant congregation included a name, a geographically defined collection of members, a resident pastor, a meeting place, a governing board, a denominational affiliation, and Sunday morning worship. The last years of the twentieth century saw the emergence of a growing number of congregations that operate under one name, with one governing board, one staff, one budget, and two to over a hundred meeting places.[1]

Do you believe this is a passing phenomenon? Or do you believe this is an attractive alternative for creating a multicultural congregation? Or will this evolve into a strategy that places several very small congregations under the umbrella of one large church that can mobilize the required resources? Do you believe the multisite option is a possibility for your congregation?

10. How much land is required for an adequate church site? In the 1950s three acres were perceived as somewhere between adequate and extravagant for either a new mission or the relocation of an existing church. By 1975 conventional wisdom was recommending five to seven acres. In 1999 the twenty- to two-hundred-acre church site was not unusual, despite the opposition of many municipal officials who concluded that meant removing too much land from the tax rolls. What do you believe will be defined as an "adequate-sized" church site in 2030? Five acres? Ten? Twenty? Forty? Eighty? One hundred? Two hundred? Or do you expect that the twenty-first century will see a continued increase in the number of congregations, both new missions and older relocating churches, that will purchase economically obsolete commercial and industrial properties and remodel the physical facilities for use by a worshiping community? That often can be accomplished at less than one-half the cost of purchasing vacant land and constructing new buildings.

11. What do you believe is the minimum size in the year 2000 for a Protestant congregation in the United States to be able to both afford and justify, in terms of the workload and the challenges, a full-time, resident, fully credentialed, and competent pastor? An average worship attendance of 75? 100? 125? 150? 170? 200?

12. Do you believe that every Christian congregation can and should mobilize the resources required to welcome and serve everyone? Or do you believe it is legitimate for congregations to carve out a distinctive niche that enables them to be responsive to the religious and personal needs of a small slice of the population?

If you believe every congregation should be prepared to offer a relevant and meaningful response to the religious and personal needs of nearly everyone living within a mile or two or three of the meeting place, how large do you believe that congregation must be to mobilize the required resources? An average worship attendance of 100? 200? 350? 700? 1,000? 1,800? 3,500? 5,000? 10,000?

13. Do you believe that the best road to the racial integration of the churches will be to place the primary emphasis on encouraging American-born blacks to join predominantly Anglo congregations? Or should the primary emphasis be on encouraging white churchgoers to join predominantly African American churches? Or to organize new multiethnic missions?

14. Do you believe the churchgoers born after 1980 will prefer the acoustic sound or the electronic sound in instrumental music?

15. Do you believe the churchgoers born after 1985 will prefer classical Christian music in worship? Or what is now called "contemporary Christian music"?

16. In many Protestant traditions the Sunday morning worship service has shrunk in length during the past 200 years from over 3 hours to 2 hours to 40 to 75 minutes. Do you believe Sunday morning worship services in the twenty-first century will be longer or shorter than they are now?

17. What do you believe will be the future in American Protestantism of highly liturgical worship that is rooted in Western European religious tradition?

18. Do you believe the geographical proximity of a congregation's meeting place to its place of residence will be one of the three most influential variables in the decision by adults in the year 2025 as they seek a new church home? Will geographical proximity be more or less influential than the denominational affiliation? More or less influential than the personality and preaching of the pastor? More or less influential than the availability of off-street parking?

19. The 1950s and 1960s popularized the goal that a theological school should be "ecumenical, urban, and university related." Do you believe those three values should drive the design of theological education in the twenty-first century? Or do you believe theological schools should place a high priority on transmitting to future parish pastors the denominational history, values, culture, belief system, and priorities? Do you believe that can be accomplished most effectively in an academic context? Or in the context of a worshiping community that draws participants from all walks of life?

20. The 1990s demonstrated that distance learning will be a growing part of the American educational system. One version brings the teacher(s) and classroom to where the students live and/or work. Another version is distance learning via the Internet and modern technology with the students and teachers located in a variety of places. Do you believe distance learning will radically change the setting for theological education in the twenty-first century?

21. Do you believe the norm for preparing candidates for the parish ministry in the twenty-first century will be (a) the current German university model, organized largely around academic departments (Bible, church history, theology, etc.), that focuses on the knowledge the student should learn or (b) a model based on the central purposes of a worshiping community (worship, fellowship, spiritual growth, evangelism, community outreach and service, pastoral care, and learning) and designed to equip future staff members, both lay and ordained, with the competencies required to fulfill those purposes?[2]

If you choose the second alternative, do you believe today's theological schools can and should be transformed from the university model into the church model? Or do you believe a more realistic strategy would be to place the responsibility for equipping the next generation of ministers and program staff members in (a) teaching churches using the church model or (b) single-function centers, each specializing in one of the seven functions identified in the previous paragraph, or (c) newly created centers, each equipping candidates in all the functions?

Or do you believe one group of centers should be designed to equip people planning to spend their careers as volunteers or as part-time paid staff in small congregations, another group of centers should be designed to prepare people to serve congregations averaging 100 to 350 at worship, a third set of centers should be designed to equip people to serve large congregations, and perhaps a half dozen centers should be designed to equip people to serve in very large congregations?

Or do you believe each congregation should enlist its future paid staff out of its own constituency and customize in-service training experiences for those individuals?

22. What do you believe is the definition of a long pastorate? Five years? Seven to ten years? Ten to fifteen years? Fifteen to twenty years? At least twenty years?

23. Some congregations project high expectations of anyone who seeks to become a full member. These usually include regular participation in the weekly corporate worship of God, involvement in a weekly Bible study group, and service as a trained volunteer. Other churches project more modest expectations of members. Which of these two types of congregations do you believe will be most attractive to the churchgoers born after 1985?

24. One approach to youth ministries is designed to be staffed largely with adult volunteers who also serve as respected and attractive role models of a committed Christian. Another approach is based on peer leadership and calls for most of the "hands-on" leadership roles to be filled by a select group of trained teenage volunteers. Which approach do you believe is better with the youth born after 1985?

25. In planning for construction of a new worship center, the leaders of the very large churches have three basic choices. One is to design one very large room that will seat 70 to 100 percent of all worshipers on the typical weekend. That is compatible with a schedule that calls for most people to worship at the same time in the same place every weekend. A second option is to design a room that will accommodate 35 to 50 percent of the weekly worship attendance. That is compatible with a schedule that calls for three or four worship experiences every weekend. A third alternative is to assume that two or three rooms will be needed for worship. One will be designed for a presentation type of worship service. One will accommodate a participatory style of worship. A third may be a room that also can serve as a chapel, a general-purpose meeting room, and a classroom. It can be designed to convey the impression of a "full house" with 75 worshipers or with 150 worshipers, but it also can be arranged to accommodate as many as 300.

Which of these three options do you believe will be appropriate for the majority of very large churches in 2025?

26. What do you believe is the most promising road to a better tomorrow for children and youth born into and reared in an urban, poverty-stricken neighborhood? Basketball or a heavily used library card?

27. Crossroads Church was founded in 1980 and now averages 1,900 at worship. The founding pastor has announced his retirement effective in six months. What do you believe should be the plan of succession: (a) invite the 42-year-old senior associate minister of a similar congregation that now averages 2,800 at worship, (b) bring in an intentional interim minister to serve for 12 to 18 months, (c) call the exceptionally gifted 33-year-old founding pastor of an eight-year-old congregation that now averages 800 at worship, or (d) "promote" the 36-year-old senior associate pastor at Crossroads Church who joined this staff seven years ago and now preaches at two of the five weekend services on 46 weekends of the year?

28. What do you believe will be extremely valuable ministries that the very large churches will help pioneer and/or perfect during the next dozen years? Charter schools? Home Bible study via an interactive web site? Off-campus ministries? Planting new missions designed to become megachurches? Training the next generation of parish pastors and program staff? Partnerships with an overseas congregation with one staff responsible for both locations and a regular exchange of volunteer leaders? Prayer groups via the Internet with members from several states, including a few who moved away but want to continue with the same prayer partners? Retreat centers? Retirement villages? A replacement for the traditional children's Sunday school organized around individualized and interactive learning opportunities using the Internet and/or CD-ROMs? Serving as a resource center to provide trained volunteers to staff small congregations?

29. During the past decade every year has set a new record for the number of intercultural marriages. What do you believe will be the consequence of this trend for what have been predominantly single-culture congregations?

30. As you plan for the next decade, what do you believe will be the most useful way to conceptualize the staffing configuration for your congregation?

The typical small church usually places a premium on skills in interpersonal relationships. The large congregations tend to focus on staffing functions, such as worship, education, youth ministries, administration, music, evangelism, pastoral care, and community outreach.

The leaders in the most intentional of the very large churches first decide on their identity. Do we see ourselves as one big extended family? Or as a congregation of classes, choirs, cells, circles, committees, fellowships, organizations, task forces, and specialized ministries? Or as a congregation of congregations of classes, choirs, circles, etc.? Or as a congregation of communities? After that decision has been made, it will be relatively easy to design the appropriate staff configuration and to enlist the individuals and teams who will be compatible with and supportive of that design.

If your leaders can agree on the responses to these and similar questions about the changing context for ministry, it will be easier to reach agreement on whether the Lord is calling your congregation to accept the role of a megachurch.

Notes

INTRODUCTION

1. For an explanation of middle-sized group dynamics, see Lyle E. Schaller, *44 Questions for Congregational Self-Appraisal* (Nashville: Abingdon Press, 1998) 172-77.

1. CULTURE, SIZE, AND CERTAINTY

1. Thomas E. Ricks, *Making the Corps* (New York: Scribner's, 1997) 19-22.
2. Ibid., 20.
3. For a discussion of how urban reformers attempted to transform the rural church, see James H. Madison, "Reformers and the Rural Church, 1900–1950," *The Journal of American History* 73 (1996) 645-68.
4. Lyle E. Schaller, *Looking in the Mirror* (Nashville: Abingdon Press, 1984) 14-37.
5. For that discussion, see Lyle E. Schaller, *The Middlesized Church* (Nashville: Abingdon Press, 1985).
6. Schaller, *Looking in the Mirror*, 27-37.
7. Leith Anderson, "The Large Church: Size Isn't Everything," *The Clergy Journal* (March 1998) 12-13.
8. For two arguments from different perspectives on ambiguity, see Peter L. Berger, "Protestantism and the Quest for Certainty," *The Christian Century*, August 26–September 2, 1998, 782-96; and Ralph C. Wood, "In Defense of Disbelief," *First Things*, October 1998, 28-33. For a historical description of the rise of agnosticism, see James Turner, *Without God, Without Creed* (Baltimore: Johns Hopkins University Press, 1985).

2. A LARGER CONTEXT

1. A more detailed and extensive discussion of the changes in the context for ministry is Lyle E. Schaller, *Discontinuity and Hope: Radical Change and the Path to the Future* (Nashville: Abingdon Press, 1999).
2. A provocative analysis of the numerical decline of the mainline Protestant denominations is Roger Finke and Rodney Stark, *The Churching of America 1776–1990* (New Brunswick, N.J.: Rutgers University Press, 1992).
3. For a thorough analysis of three significant movements under that broad umbrella of "Made in America" Christian bodies, see Donald E. Miller, *Reinventing American Protestantism* (Berkeley: University of California Press, 1997). A more extensive description of "Made in

America" religious traditions is Paul K. Conkin, *American Originals* (Chapel Hill: University of North Carolina Press, 1997).

4. Mark Edmundson, "On the Uses of a Liberal Education," *Harper's Magazine*, September 1997, 43.

5. My first attempt to call attention to this trend was in a brief monograph, "The Coming Crisis in New Church Development," published by the Regional Church Planning Office, Cleveland, Ohio, 1967. A longer historical summary can be found in Lyle E. Schaller, *44 Questions for Church Planters* (Nashville: Abingdon Press, 1991) 14-21.

6. See *Media Studies Journal* (Fall 1998) for a series of insightful reflections on that tumultuous year.

7. A brief summary of this debate is offered by Richard Morin, "Finding the Smoking Gun," *Washington Post*, National Weekly Edition, November 9, 1998, 34.

8. The loss of a geographically defined sense of community in urban America is lamented in a superb book, Alan Ehrenhalt, *The Lost City* (New York: Basic Books, 1995).

9. A superb description of the fundamentalism of the 1930s and 1940s, written from a later perspective, is Joel A. Carpenter, *Revive Us Again* (New York: Oxford University Press, 1997). See also an interesting brief for lifting up grace over law in Ellen Charry, *By the Renewing of Your Minds* (New York: Oxford University Press, 1998). The argument that pluralism is a fertile context for the growth of contemporary evangelicalism is made by Christian Smith, *American Evangelicalism: Embattered and Thriving* (Chicago: University of Chicago Press, 1998).

10. Joel Perlmann and Roger Waldinger, "Are the Children of Today's Immigrants Making It?" *The Public Interest* (Summer 1998) 73-96. See also Matthew Frye Jacobson, *Whiteness of a Different Color* (Cambridge, Mass.: Harvard University Press, 1998) for a discussion of the changing definition of "race" in America and the implications for the assimilation of the children and grandchildren of immigrants of Latin American, Asian, and African American descent. For an exceptionally useful long-term perspective on the consequences of immigration, see Thomas Sowell, *Migrations and Cultures* (New York: Basic Books, 1996). The current public policy debate over the Americanization of immigrants is summarized by Mark Kirkorian, "Will Americanization Work in America," *Freedom Review* (Fall 1997) 45-53.

11. Up through the 1990s, female parish pastors were found in disproportionately large numbers in small and middle-sized congregations. See Patricia M. Y. Chang, "Paying the Preacher Her Due," in William B. Lawrence et al., eds., *The People(s) Called Methodist* (Nashville: Abingdon Press, 1998) 163-65.

Notes

3. THE CONSEQUENCES OF CONSUMERISM

1. James Miller, "The Academy Writes Back," *Lingua Franca* (March 1997) 60.
2. Mark Edmundson, "On the Uses of a Liberal Education," *Harper's Magazine*, September 1997, 39-49.
3. For a carefully thought-out critique of consumer capitalism, see Rodney Clapp, "Why the Devil Takes Visa," *Christianity Today*, October 7, 1996, 19-33. In recent years several European economists have restated the heart of the issue. Instead of framing the question in terms of the power of the producer versus the power of the consumer, they contend that the real issue is free markets (choice and competition) versus a more egalitarian distribution of income and wealth. Elmar Altwater in Germany; Vivianne Forrestier, Jean-Paul Fitoussi, and Pierre Bourdieu in France; and Anthony Giddens in England are among the most influential critics of free market consumerism.
4. John A. Jackle et al., *The Motel in America* (Baltimore: Johns Hopkins University Press, 1996) 57-230.
5. The argument that the Port Huron Statement was an exceptionally influential critique is made by Eric Foner, *The Story of American Freedom* (New York: W. W. Norton & Company, 1998) 289-99.
6. A more contemporary, and also very sympathetic interpretation, of the Port Huron Statement is in Alan Adelson, *SDS* (New York: Charles Scribner's Sons, 1972) 206-8. A series of insightful essays on the tumultuous year of 1968 by journalists of that era, but written from the perspective of the late 1990s, can be found in *Media Studies Journal* (Fall 1998).
7. This observer's reaction to *Baker v. Carr* can be found in Lyle E. Schaller, *The Tensions of Reapportionment* (New York: National Council of Churches, 1965).
8. Andrew C. Reukin, "As Need for Food Grows, Donations Steadily Drop," *New York Times*, February 27, 1999.
9. This influx of profit-making corporations into the nonprofit world is described in William P. Ryan, "The New Landscape of Nonprofits," *Harvard Business Review* (January-February 1999) 127-36.
10. Lyle E. Schaller, *44 Ways to Expand the Financial Base of Your Congregation* (Nashville: Abingdon Press, 1989) 49-81.
11. For a brief on behalf of a denominational affirmation of theological pluralism, see Peter L. Berger, "Protestantism and the Quest for Certainty," *The Christian Century*, August 26–September 2, 1998, 782-96.
12. Ray Oldenburg, *The Great Good Place* (New York: Paragon House, 1991).
13. Ibid.

4. WHY SO FEW?

1. The multisite option is described in Lyle E. Schaller, *Innovations in Ministry* (Nashville: Abingdon Press, 1994) 112-33.
2. Many years ago an economist declared that five of the great democracies in the history of the Western world came to an end by vote of the people. Willis J. Ballinger, *By Vote of the People* (New York: Charles Scribner's Sons, 1946). The central thesis of that book helps to explain why congregations that require approval at a congregational meeting of all policy decisions rarely exceed an average worship attendance of 800.
3. James D. Glasse, *Putting It Together in the Parish* (Nashville: Abingdon Press, 1972) 53-61.
4. For suggestions on planned change, see Lyle E. Schaller, *The Change Agent* (Nashville: Abingdon Press, 1977).

5. LEADERSHIP ROLES

1. For a discussion on how the culture and size of a congregation influence the members' expectations of the pastor's role, see Lyle E. Schaller, *Looking in the Mirror* (Nashville: Abingdon Press, 1984) 14-37.
2. Henry Mintzberg, "Covert Leadership: Notes on Managing Professionals," *Harvard Business Review* (November-December 1998) 140-47. This essay should be read by the senior minister of every large church.
3. Thomas Bender, *Intellect and Public Life* (Baltimore: Johns Hopkins University Press, 1993) 127-39.
4. A fascinating research report on how leaders shape the culture and the institutional environment of a theological school is Jackson W. Carroll et al., *Being There* (New York: Oxford University Press, 1997).
5. Rolf Memming, "United Methodist Ordained Ministry in Transition," in *The People(s) Called Methodist*, ed. William B. Lawrence et al. (Nashville: Abingdon Press, 1998) 142-46.

7. RESERVATIONS AND QUESTIONS

1. A discussion of the conflict created by organizing against the enemy can be found in Lyle E. Schaller, *Community Organization: Conflict and Reconciliation* (Nashville: Abingdon Press, 1966) 49-114.
2. Richard L. Dunagin, *Beyond These Walls* (Nashville: Abingdon Press, 1999) 39-45.
3. Edward C. Banfield, *The Unheavenly City* (Boston: Little, Brown and Company, 1968); Edward C. Banfield, *The Unheavenly City Revisited* (Boston: Little, Brown and Company, 1974).
4. For a powerful brief on behalf of indigenous leadership, see J. V. Thomas and J. Timothy Ahlen, *One Church, Many Congregations* (Nashville: Abingdon Press, 1999).

5. For two contrasting views on the involvement of congregations in urban affairs, see Arthur E. Farneley II, "Can Churches Save the City? A Look at Resources," *The Christian Century*, December 9, 1998, 1182-84; and John J. Dilulio Jr., "The Lord's Word," *The Brookings Review* (Fall 1997) 27-31.
6. Robert L. Randall, *What People Expect from Church* (Nashville: Abingdon Press, 1992).
7. Tom Brokaw, *The Greatest Generation* (New York: Random House, 1998).
8. See Lyle E. Schaller, *Tattered Trust* (Nashville: Abingdon Press, 1996) 49-61.
9. An operational step in the process of strengthening local leadership is described in Charles M. Olsen, *Transforming Church Boards into Communities of Spiritual Leaders* (Washington, D.C.: The Alban Institute, 1995).

8. A DENOMINATIONAL PERSPECTIVE

1. David Shearer, "Outsourcing War," *Foreign Policy* (Fall 1998) 73.
2. P. J. Simmons, "Learning to Live with NGOS," *Foreign Policy* (Fall 1998) 82-96.
3. Ibid., 87.
4. A useful brief discussion of the growing impact of N.G.O.s is Paul Lewis, "It's Not Just Governments That Make War and Peace Now," *New York Times*, November 28, 1998.
5. A favorable account of the history and role of parachurch organizations is Jerry White, *The Church and the Parachurch* (Portland, Ore.: Multnomah Press, 1983). A more recent book estimates the number of parachurch organizations may be close to 100,000. Wesley K. Willmer, J. David Schmidt, and Martyn Smith, *The Prospering Parachurch: Enlarging the Boundaries of God's Kingdom* (San Francisco: Jossey-Bass, 1998).
6. An excellent introduction to the centuries-old debate over trust is David Boldt, "Do We Still Trust the Common Man?" *Philanthropy* (January-February, 1999) 22-27. For a more extensive discussion, see Christopher Lasch, *The Revolt of the Masses* (New York: W. W. Norton & Company, 1995).
7. The quotation from Clint Bolick can be found in Boldt, "Do We Still Trust the Common Man?" 27.

9. WHAT DO YOU BELIEVE?

1. The best introduction to off-campus ministries is by J. Timothy Ahlen and J V Thomas, *One Church, Many Congregations* (Nashville: Abingdon Press, 1999) 17-45.
2. I am indebted to a brilliant essay by J. Sam Simmons, "The Truly Innovative Seminary," for this distinction between the academic model and the church model for theological schools.